Be a Happy Leader

BE A HAPPY LEADER BOOK BLURBS

Being a Happy Leader is a lifelong quest for us all. Tia lays out her personal experiences which inspired her to inspire the rest of us. Her stories are infused with research, training, and personal anecdotes. She challenges your mindset and provides tools to become happier at work and home.

Carla Murray, President, U.S. Western
Region Full-Service, Marriott

In the 21st century, it is essential for leaders to consider their own wellbeing as well as that of their employees. Increasing organizational wellbeing leads to higher levels of creativity and productivity, as well as motivation and engagement--all precursors to better performance. This is why Tia Graham's book is so important. By weaving research and storytelling, theory and practice, Tia presents a blueprint for personal and organizational flourishing.

Dr. Tal Ben-Shahar, *New York Times* Bestselling Author
of *Happier*, Founder of The Happiness Studies Academy
and Past Professor at Harvard University

Tia has consistently been one of the highest rated, most motivating speakers we have had. Her insights on the impacts that physical well-being, healthy habits and a happy outlook can have on empathetic leadership are both refreshing and thought provoking. A fantastic methodology to learn more about the power that positive thinking can have on your leadership journey.

Geoff Ballotti, President and CEO, Wyndham Hotels & Resorts

Be a Happy Leader is a refreshing, must-read book for any leader hoping to create a world-class team with breakout results while also maintaining a healthy focus on their personal life. Tia's emphasis on measuring and celebrating what matters is one of the most important drivers of success and a message that I routinely reinforce with my portfolio companies. Entrepreneurs must constantly overcome seemingly insurmountable obstacles to make their dream a reality, and *Be a Happy Leader* reminds us that we can all tap into our full potential by prioritizing well-being and a positive mindset.

Mamoon Hamid, Partner at Kleiner Perkins

This book could not have arrived at a better time. Tia combines her passion for people, world experience and her understanding of science into the manual for successful leadership that will redefine the way you live life, both professionally and personally. It's like having a joyful business coach in your pocket.

Nicole Elice, Vice President – Entertainment Publicity Showtime Networks

Tia Graham has written a book which is both remarkably valuable and a pleasure to read. In every chapter, leaders will find in-depth wisdom combined with practical examples, all written in a style that is both authentic and inviting. Reading this book will make you a better leader, and best of all, you'll enjoy the journey.

Jim Huling, #1 *Wall Street Journal* Best Selling Author and Global Consultant, *The 4 Disciplines of Execution*

Tia Graham has discovered the power and beauty of living a purposeful, passionate life—which means a happy life—and she shares her discoveries with us. Her recommendations—to reclaim the joy you knew as a child, to stay connected with your passion, to honor yourself, and to stay connected to others—will not only lead to happiness; they'll also lead to better health. I hope everyone will read *Be a Happy Leader* and make the decision to Arrive At Happy for themselves and their teams.

Dr. Howard Murad, Founder of MURAD Cosmetics and Author of *Conquering Cultural Stress*

Tia Graham brings happiness to leaders, teams, and organizations, and once you read this book and follow her practical methodology, you too can elevate yourself and everyone around you. As someone who has been leading the global happiness at work efforts for almost 20 years, I just know that you will find great value in this book.

Alexander Kjerulf, Founder, Woo Hoo Inc. and Author of *Leading with Happiness* and *Happy Hour is 9 to 5*

In an era of uncertainty and change, appreciation, care, and a sense of purpose and happiness become all the more critical in today's workplace. Tia Graham captures the essence of happiness and leading teams through her personal journey and applies it masterfully. Effective leadership starts with the journey to uncover oneself. *Be a Happy Leader* delivers the happiness fuel you need to propel you into becoming the leader you've always wanted to be.

Larry Levine, Best Selling Author of *Selling From the Heart* and Co-Host of the Selling From the Heart podcast

Hiring and retaining the best leaders and teams is paramount to our success in hospitality, housing, and mixed-use real estate properties. Tia's 8-step methodology gives leaders a proven roadmap to grow their business by creating winning cultures. Tia had tremendous impact during her time at The W Istanbul hotel, and every leader will be inspired by her perspective.

Serdar Bilgili, Chairman, Bilgili Holding and BLG Capital

Be a Happy Leader is a motivating read for business development leaders who want to move their businesses forward, increase sales and create happy, loyal teams. Her evidence-based strategies and 8-step method are exactly what busy, working parents like myself need today. I recommend that you read this book with your leadership group and integrate her tactics into your culture. Not only will you realize business growth, but each person will have more enjoyment in their life and work - which we all need!

Shelly Cayette, SVP, Global Partnerships, Cleveland Cavaliers

Having grown up in the hospitality business with Tia, I have seen firsthand how she has taken her incredible leadership skills and science research and applied them to this book and her ultimate goal of happiness for all. This book is transformational and a guide for all of us to truly find happiness in our day to day. Tia makes this feel attainable with her 8-step methodology and incredible energy throughout this book.

Katharine Jerkens, SVP, Global Sales & Marketing
Uncle Nearest, Inc.

BE A
HAPPY
LEADER

Stop Feeling Overwhelmed, Thrive Personally,
and Achieve Killer Business Results

Tia Graham

Founder, Arrive At Happy

NEW YORK

LONDON • NASHVILLE • MELBOURNE • VANCOUVER

BE A HAPPY LEADER

Stop Feeling Overwhelmed, Thrive Personally, and Achieve Killer Business Results

© 2022 Tia Graham

Published in New York, New York, by Morgan James Publishing. Morgan James is a trademark of Morgan James, LLC. www.MorganJamesPublishing.com

Proudly distributed by Ingram Publisher Services.

A FREE ebook edition is available for you or a friend with the purchase of this print book.

CLEARLY SIGN YOUR NAME ABOVE

Instructions to claim your free ebook edition:
1. Visit MorganJamesBOGO.com
2. Sign your name CLEARLY in the space above
3. Complete the form and submit a photo of this entire page
4. You or your friend can download the ebook to your preferred device

ISBN 9781631955907 paperback
ISBN 9781631955914 ebook
Library of Congress Control Number: 2021935767

Cover and Interior Design by:
Chris Treccani
www.3dogcreative.net

Morgan James is a proud partner of Habitat for Humanity Peninsula and Greater Williamsburg. Partners in building since 2006.

Get involved today! Visit MorganJamesPublishing.com/giving-back

DEDICATION

For the leaders of teams around the globe
who care and want to make a difference.

May you commit to your own joy, be a positive force
in your organization, and create a ripple effect
wherever you lead.

TABLE OF CONTENTS

ACKNOWLEDGMENTS

Never have I felt as much purpose and meaning as when I am speaking and teaching leaders, teams, and individuals how to be more successful through happiness. My intention for this book was to touch as many lives as possible and be a catalyst in changing how work happens. Many people have supported me in my journey, and because of them, *Be a Happy Leader* was made possible.

I would like to thank my husband, James Gancos, for your unwavering encouragement for my work and mission. You have always been my biggest cheerleader and believed in the mission of Arrive At Happy from day one. My mother, Claudia Hardy, and my father, Peter Graham, for giving me a loving and adventurous childhood that enabled me to thrive personally and become who I was meant to be. Thank you for your consistent encouragement, grounding advice, connection to Mother Nature, enjoying life, and family connection. Thank you to my sisters, Helen Hailey Graham and Stephanie Graham, for your friendship, guidance, and the endless laughter. My journey is rich and complete with both of you by my side.

Thank you to my dear friend and coach, Cherie Healey, for your fire and zest! Your support empowered me to create Arrive At Happy, believe in my vision, and to always stay connected to my heart and soul. I would like to acknowledge my colleague, Angela

Vento, for believing in me at such a young age and promoting me to become a leader of people as I began my career. You saw more in me than I saw in myself at that time and started me on a path to truly soar. Thank you to Corinne Janssen, Denise Wardlow, Darren Green, Ozlem Goksin, Leon Young, Dan King, Tim Ananiadis, and Jeff Kulek for exemplifying outstanding leadership, and for your positive influence on my professional life.

I would like to acknowledge Dr. Tal Ben-Shahar for his inspiration, education, and passion for positive psychology, and for being a vital part of the happiness revolution. Thank you to Karen Guggenheim for your hard work and dedication in creating and building the global community with the World Happiness Summit and the WOHASU Foundation.

My book partner, Ashley Mansour, I appreciate you so much, and, without you, this book wouldn't have been possible. Karen Anderson and David. L. Hancock from Morgan James Publishing, thank you for believing in this book and my mission.

My love and appreciation to my daughters, Mackenzie and Audrey, for being my newest and very powerful teachers. You are the catalyst for my happiness work, and challenge me to be a better human being every single day.

ADDITIONAL RESOURCES

You have chosen to prioritize yourself and your team, and you are passionate about achieving results with purpose. Because I cannot be with you in person, I have created the Be A Happy Leader Resource Center to support you on your journey. Your success in life and in leadership depends on your motivation, but even more so on the actions you take daily. This book offers many strategies and practical tactics that I have personally used. In the online Resource Center, you will find videos and resources that I personally recommend to all of my clients, in addition to downloadable assets to ensure the inspiration turns into powerful action. I recommend that you download the digital assets now and utilize them as you read this book. You can access tools to use for your personal life, your career, and with your team. The global happiness revolution is happening, and it's my mission to create as many happy leaders as possible! The positive ripple effect to society and business is extraordinary.

Access the Be A Happy Leader Resource Center:
www.arriveathappy.com/happy-leader-resources

ARRIVE AT HAPPY

NOTE FROM THE AUTHOR

To respect the privacy of friends and colleagues and to maintain client confidentiality, I have altered various personal details.

FOREWORD
By Karen Guggenheim,
Founder WOHASU®, World Happiness Summit®

Tia Graham inspires us in *Be a Happy Leader* to go beyond our biology and biases to have the courage to learn how to lead a life in a more meaningful way, personally and professionally. In her book, she shares her methodology on how to use the science of happiness to teach readers how to embrace positive and lasting change by using tools and activities to rewire our brains. She carefully lays down the groundwork for the worthy pursuit of happiness and cautions against the costs of letting unhappiness and unchecked stress impact every facet of our lives. She is a firm believer of what is possible, and of what leadership can look like and what it can achieve by cultivating leaders who are positive and optimistic.

Tia's purpose in writing *Be a Happy Leader* is to inspire people who are leading but are not feeling fulfilled. Her message to leaders around the world is that optimal leadership begins by placing your own happiness first.

Tia's story begins with her personal passion and quest to make people happy. She incorporates her many talents, experience leading teams, infectious energy, and love for learning to fuel her quest. I first met her at the World Happiness Summit® (WOHASU) in 2018, where she acted as a facilitator and WOHASU® coach. There she led group discussions that supported the WOHASU mission of spreading happiness to a global audience. In 2019, I asked her to speak and share her story about creating *Arrive at Happy*. She went on to become certified as a happiness trainer through the Happiness Studies Academy and as a chief happiness officer.

In *Be a Happy Leader*, Tia brings together her happiness research and training, in addition to her years of leadership experience in the hospitality industry to teach leaders how to attain happiness and business results. She uses science to support premises that we know intuitively and provides us with a practical guide to become happier both in our personal and work lives, for there can be no distinction as we are the same person both at work and at home. This is even more so now, as the boundaries that previously protected home life has evaporated.

We need a book like *Be a Happy Leader* now more than ever because technology has afforded us great opportunities and conveniences, yet it has made us available around the clock. Globalization has increasingly connected us to a global community, but this interconnectedness and access to constant information comes at a cost. Stress, the feeling of being overwhelmed, and anxiety are currently at record levels.

Tia explains how we operate within ourselves and our social circles and work communities. In taking a research-based approach, she gently demystifies the frameworks causing us to act the way that we do and offers the necessary knowledge for change. Some people are walking other people's paths; we must have the courage to find our own. In her book's early chapters, she lays the foundation for readers to connect with their self-knowledge to acquire self-awareness. By creating a safe space for introspection, Tia then delves into the eight steps of the methodology that forms the crux of *Be a Happy Leader*.

Be a Happy Leader flows from personal stories to science, taking a practical and commonsense approach. Tia's voice is enthusiastic, genuine, and encouraging throughout. This is a book that you will highlight, reread, and share. Practical nuggets of information can be found everywhere in this book, based on positive psychology and neuroscience, which is what every happy and successful leader needs.

CHAPTER 1:
The Calling of Leadership

What if you could create sustainable happiness and lifelong contentment? How many lives and careers could you positively impact if you had an exact methodology for success?

Do you wonder if you're on the right leadership career path? Do you feel overwhelmed, stressed, and unsure if you have what it takes to be an incredible leader who is filled with joy and purpose?

I have been in that very situation several times throughout my 15-year career as a team leader. At a very young age, I was thrown into the water to sink or swim, so to speak, and became a leader. I was promoted by one of my mentors to be a director of sales and marketing at the age of twenty-six after being a manager for only one year. That mentor and others ensured that I did not drown, and I worked my tail off to make sure that I kept swimming. I led my first team to many successes, and I learned a lot of what not to do from that first role as well.

Deep down, I have always known that I wanted to be happy and enjoy life. I have also known that I truly enjoy working with and inspiring people, and that I was born to lead others. You might feel similarly. Just like every other leader, I have experienced the roller coaster of ups and downs throughout life. Along the way, I have learned and discovered incredible insights and strategies, and I am here to share them with you.

Happiness

You can absolutely create sustainable happiness in both your personal and professional life. By happiness, I don't mean being filled with excitement, love, and joy every second of every day—it isn't humanly possible. Every single human on this earth feels pain via stress, anger, fear, guilt, and sadness. What I mean by happiness is a commitment to your personal joy, contentment, and purpose while accepting the peaks and valleys of life. Happiness at life is about being resilient and appreciating all the incredible gifts that life has to offer. Happiness at work is knowing that you're on the right path and working towards purposeful goals. It's understanding that your work matters and that you make a difference. When you're happy at work, you use your personal strengths and truly connect with those with whom you work. Again, it isn't possible to be in a happy state every single day when you're at work. However, when you are content while working, your good days outnumber the challenging ones, and the pleasant emotions outnumber the unpleasant feelings on average.

Everyone must work with difficult people every day. Currently, you might be dealing with a very distressing boss. Your peers and stakeholders might make you want to scream. Some of your direct reports might irritate you because they are your exact opposite, leaving you feeling that they're misaligned or not on the same page as you at all. Dealing with such people drains your energy. Office politics exists in every organization. As a result, you must balance your own beliefs and conviction while continuously working on building and maintaining relationships with all those surrounding you.

The Demands of Leadership

As a leader in an organization, you might feel some, or all, of these emotions in your professional life right now: overwhelmed, overworked, unbalanced, uninspired, frustrated, and stressed. Are you unsure if you're moving in the right direction with your career and your life overall? Have you landed in an industry where you're unsure if it's the right one for you? Do you find it challenging to align your team in order to exceed your annual targets? Maybe you wish you were living a healthier life. Are you stressed about your financial situation and wish that you had more money? Do you not get along with one or more colleagues, stakeholders, or maybe even your boss? It's likely you simply want to be happier at work!

I understand the feeling of spinning your wheels for days, weeks, and months on end, not knowing when you will come up for air. I know how frustrating it is to work long hours and still not achieve the team results that you want and need. When the leadership challenges you face outweigh the number of successes you have, you might feel as if you are running on a hamster wheel—a very tiring and soul-crushing hamster wheel. When you put a tremendous amount of effort into your leadership role and don't move forward at the speed you want and need, it's frustrating and energy-depleting. Throughout this book, I will share several personal stories to show that you are not alone, and that you will *never* be alone.

As a leader striving for excellence and results, you likely feel acute pressure in life. You don't want to disappoint your boss, the stakeholders, your peers, your team, your family, your friends, and, above all, yourself. The fear that you feel about not being successful in a leadership role can weigh very heavily on you. Throughout my leadership career, I've had days when I questioned, "Am I the right person for this job? Am I good enough?" Leaders spend time, effort, and resources studying, training, working, and building relationships so that they can become a team leader with large responsibilities.

As a Type A person with a tendency towards perfectionism, I didn't want my loving and supportive parents to see me fail. The thought of disappointing my parents, myself, and, later on, my direct bosses kept me working long hours into the night on a weekly basis. As an adult, I chose a leadership career in sales and marketing. The stress of doing well and achieving goals has always been a constant in my adult life.

Being a leader today means juggling expectations, teams, technology, and never-ending demands. The volume of work can be overwhelming, the to-do list is continuously growing, and leaders are expected to always be available due to perpetually evolving technology and the glorification of "busy." As a leader, you must constantly navigate office bureaucracy, which can slow you down or even bring you to a complete stop. It can be difficult to focus between 9:00 A.M. and 6:00 P.M. due to the overwhelming quantity of meetings, phone calls, and pop-up emergencies. Trying to balance being supportive and available for your team while moving your projects and work forward can be difficult, especially when you're distracted by news, social media, text messages, email, and phone calls. Toss in dealing with demands from your boss, peers, stakeholders, and team members, and your daily work life can become overwhelming. It is likely rare, indeed, when you can find an hour to focus on a project in peace.

Is it a struggle to motivate, inspire, and retain your star team members? Do you worry that they may leave at some point in the near future? Or perhaps it has already occurred. Has one of your very best employees recently resigned, only to be hired by a competitor? Whenever that happens, physical, emotional, and psychological energy is sucked right out of your body, mind, and spirit. As a passionate and engaged leader, having the right people in the right positions moving forward together fills you with energy for your work. It is detrimental when a valued team member goes to a competitor because it lowers the morale of the team, sets you back in terms of productivity, and is costly to recruit, hire, and train a new team member.

Are several members on your team mediocre? Are they showing up and working but are nowhere near giving it their all? Do they have what it takes to transform into star team members? Some may simply not be the right fit, perhaps inherited from your predecessor's team, leaving you to wonder how they lasted so long in the organization. You might be unsure how, when, and if you can even manage to remove ineffective people from your team. Perhaps it's daunting to fathom even recruiting and hiring anyone better.

Your given goals could be unrealistic. So, not only are you thinking, "How am I ever going to achieve them?" but your mind could also be filled with thoughts like "How am I going to convince my team that we can achieve these goals?"

Personal Well-Being

Right now, happiness and purpose in your personal life and work are needed more than ever. Personal well-being is crucial to successful and impactful leadership. Without it, it's extremely hard for a leader to become the person that they've envisioned. Work has always challenged team leaders, but nowadays additional obstacles exist in work and personal life. Leaders are expected to surpass goals, be continuously innovative, and have high employee engagement. Tremendous value is placed on material wealth and status, and everyone must constantly drive to achieve more. We are bombarded with negative news media 24/7 via our smartphones, which creates a lifestyle where we're always distracted and receiving content whether we like it or not, no matter where we are. As the work volume grows, it becomes even more difficult to focus on what needs to be focused on.

Families are spread out geographically, and time for friendships is reduced. Grocery stores are jam-packed with prepackaged foods that are highly processed, full of sugar, and genetically modified. These foods make us think that we are happy, yet they hurt our physical bodies. The convenience of life makes it challenging to have the desire or need to move. We can receive anything with a few clicks, why we would walk anywhere? The state of the planet is depressing and feels hopeless, along with a huge laundry list of other international issues that exist. While society is more connected than ever before, it is easy and common to feel isolated in today's world. Anxiety and depression are increasing among both children and adults, yet all everyone wants to feel is happy and successful.

Do you truly want to be a thriving, accomplished leader? Do you want to put in the effort of self-discovery and professional development? Now is the time to prioritize your personal well-being and learn how to become a happy and successful leader! If not now, when?

Be A Happy Leader

I have created the *Be a Happy Leader* methodology to give you the exact strategies and tools to incorporate into your life to help you not only be happy in your personal life, but also be happy and successful in your career. Using my strategies and tactics, you can learn how to be a positive leader, to impact your direct reports and colleagues, and to achieve wildly successful business results.

My Personal Career History

Everyone must start somewhere. I began my work life as a fast-food worker at Dairy Queen and as a part-time babysitter. I also sold shoes in a department store and collected lift tickets at a ski resort. At the age of 18, I was fired from my job at a pizza restaurant because I was ill-suited for the position at the time and did not take it seriously. It was a great lesson for me. I learned that if you are not serious about a position, there are real consequences, and I felt the embarrassment of not succeeding at a role.

Some of my bosses have been inspirational and strong, while others have been demoralizing and manipulative. My physical work environments have been both extremely ugly and energy-sucking to really beautiful and calming. Some members of my teams have had attitudes, personality conflicts, and have made judgment errors. Some of my team members have been the strongest and most incredible people that I've ever met. I've been stressed out and anxiety ridden. I've fumed at decisions that owners and stakeholders have made. There were many long days and even longer nights. Yet, I've always known that I wanted to be a leader and took it very seriously. I believe being a leader doesn't have to be extremely hard; it can, in fact, be a ton of fun! Know that I am here for you and with you. At times, I have questioned myself as a leader but continued on the path because of the calling to lead and inspire people.

My hope is that you live with contentment, purpose, and joy. My goal is that you are successful in all areas of your life and positively impact every single person that you lead.

Maslow's Hierarchy of Needs

When people are in a state where they're trying only to get their needs met, they are not trying to also feel happy every day. If a person doesn't have shelter or enough food to eat and is worried about personal safety, they're focused only on making decisions to meet their needs. In order for people to prioritize their personal well-being and focus on being happy, their needs must be met first. Per Abraham Maslow's "hierarchy of needs," human beings start thinking about actualizing their potential only once their basic needs are met.

Unfortunately, misconceptions and myths abound as to what makes us happy and content with our lives.

Money and Happiness

A glaring misconception is that most people believe that when they have more money, they will be happier. Since childhood, this message has been continuously reinforced by our parents, other family members, friends, and society. We receive it consistently from the media, especially social media, and via marketing messages. Various studies have been completed on happiness and money. One study showed that experiential purchases (money spent on *doing*) tend to provide more enduring happiness than material purchases (money spent on *having*). The researchers demonstrate that waiting for experiences tends to be more positive, pleasurable, and exciting than waiting for possessions.[1]

Another study demonstrated that experiential purchases enhance social relations more readily and effectively than material goods, form a bigger part of a person's identity, and are evaluated more on their own terms and evoke fewer social comparisons than material purchases.[2] It is also interesting to note that people who spend money on others report greater happiness than if they are spending it on themselves. The benefits of such prosocial spending emerge among adults around the world, and the warm glow of giving can be detected even in toddlers.[3] Martin Seligman, PhD, the "father of positive psychology," teaches about the hedonic treadmill, also known as the hedonic adaptation. A former president of the American Psychological Association, he is called the father of Positive psychology because his primary aim has been the promotion of the field of what makes humans thrive and what makes life worth living. He has spent his life expanding the research to the areas of education, health, and neuroscience.

The hedonic treadmill demonstrates that once people are living in a relatively comfortable financial position, more money does not necessarily equal a large increase in their personal happiness. For example, in the United States, when a single person is making $75,000 annually, any additional income adds only a small incremental increase in happiness. Let's say said person receives a $15,000 salary increase. What the hedonic treadmill reveals is that he'll have a spike in his pleasant emotions for three to four months, and then he'll return to his resting level of happiness—his happiness baseline. This same phenomenon occurs when a person making over the annual amount spends money to buy a new car. She'll feel her happiness and pleasant emotions increase temporarily, then she'll return to how she felt prior to the purchase.

This isn't to say that individuals shouldn't be ambitious or not want to prosper in their careers. What it does demonstrate is that financial success is not the sole path to happiness. However, young people and adults consistently receive the strong message that "if you become 'successful,' you'll be happy," which isn't necessarily the case.

Another misconception is that status, titles, and power are highly correlated with happiness. Studies show that people who are in places of wealth are slightly happier than the less fortunate, but it is marginally incremental. High income buys life satisfaction, the thoughts people have when they think about their life, but not emotional well-being, the emotional quality of an individual's everyday experience.[4] Many extremely wealthy and powerful people are miserable inside. However, if your status, title, and/or power are by-products of a personally meaningful pursuit, your happiness will definitely increase due to your purposeful journey, achieving the meaningful goals along the way, and the impact that you make.

My Happiness Mission

You might be wondering why I ventured into so much investigation about one core question: What makes people happy?

I was blessed with two loving parents and had a loving family. I was a happy-go-lucky child with a natural sunny disposition and always thrived when I was around other people. I grew up at a small local ski area in the Pine Pass in Northern British Columbia, Canada. The closest town was a 45-minute drive away, and the average temperature in the winter was -20°F. We didn't have a phone or television in our log cabin until I was 5 years old, and I took a school bus through the Rocky Mountains to elementary school. I've always felt very grateful for my experiences in life, and part of it might be due to the fact that I grew up in the middle of a forest! My parents separated when I was 10 and then divorced a few years afterward. My entire family moved to Kelowna, British Columbia, Canada, after their separation.

Like most people, I didn't have a perfect childhood. In addition to the regular challenges faced by any child, I grew up in two households. I didn't feel extremely happy as a young adult because I felt unconnected to who I was. I was very fortunate, however, to rediscover my authentic child-like happiness again in my early 20s, and I'm going to share with you exactly how I did it. I acknowledge that some people spend their entire life searching for that ease and joy experienced in childhood and that they sometimes aren't successful in locating it. I'm going to tell you exactly how I got back to that state, however, and have consciously focused on that happiness way of living throughout my life.

My Happiness Aha Moment

From my early 20s onward, people continually asked me, "How do you stay so positive? Where do you get all that energy? Even when things aren't going well, how do you feel optimistic?" My friends, coworkers, bosses, and family members have consistently inquired about how I stay so "happy." Around the age of 30, I experienced a moment of great insight and clarity: I realized that I was much happier than the average person. I knew that, whether by nature or nurture, I was able to live my life in a way that most people didn't. At the same time, I felt compelled to share this information with others. I thought to myself, "I can teach and help other people live and feel happier at work and in life." At the time, I wrote this down in my journal and shared it with a few people very close to me. From that point onward, whenever I was feeling unmotivated, frustrated, and off-purpose in my career and in my life, I would write the following in my journal:

I WILL start my happiness company! I WILL help other people live a happier life!

It was a long journey of learning what happiness really is and what elevates happiness at work before I could get to where I am today with my company, Arrive At Happy.

Let's fast-forward. At 36 years old, I was miserable and struggling emotionally at one of the lowest points in my life, and I felt completely stuck. I'd attempted to balance my executive leadership career, motherhood of two, relationships, and health, but I wasn't balancing them well and wasn't happy at all. One of my close friends recommended I speak with a life/business coach. I took the advice, and after one inspirational, hope-filled call with her, I was hooked. I told my coach about my dream of creating and running a happiness company, and she motivated me to build it. I thought I needed a life coach, but I really needed a business coach to create my new company and the lifestyle that I needed.

"What makes people happy?" was the question that I was asking myself during this time in my life. I wanted to know the answer for myself and for the organization that I was building. My research included happiness TED Talks, books, happiness experts, and life and leadership coaching. I accidentally discovered the "science of happiness" (positive psychology) and remember thinking, "What? There is a happiness science? How cool is that!"

While I was studying happiness, I came across the annual World Happiness Summit at the University of Miami and thought, "I have to attend!" Harvard's Dr. Tal Ben-Shahar, who earned his PhD in Organizational Behavior, spoke at the summit and announced his new Happiness Studies Academy and positive psychology certification programs. The Academy's courses looked extremely interesting, so I signed up right away. In the fall of 2019, I became certified in Denmark as a chief happiness officer for happiness at work. I became a certified coach with the International Coaching Federation. I created and began holding happiness workshops for the public and received extremely positive feedback from them. This feedback gave me the confidence to start selling my workshops to corporations. I realized my dream was to lead a weekend happiness retreat in Malibu, and I led 18 individuals through a transformational experience, which gave me the knowledge of how to start selling retreats to other organizations. I then became very involved in the National Speakers Association, became a board member for the Los Angeles chapter, and started giving keynote lectures. I still continue to research, study, and grow in the fields of positive psychology and happiness at work. Being a positive leader in work and in life has been my passion for a very long time, and I hope that you will gain inspiration and energy that you need by reading this book.

My Goal for the Reader

When you are finished, you will be satisfied, motivated, and armed with a toolbox of strategies and tactics to increase your personal and professional happiness, lead positively and confidently, and achieve killer business results! Are you ready? Let's begin!

Happy Leader Prompts

1. Journaling: What does Happy Leadership mean to me?
2. Journaling Activity: Write as many answers as possible to this sentence: "I feel Happy when ..."
3. Watch Dan Gilbert's TED talk, "The Surprising Science of Happiness."

CHAPTER 2:
Positive Leadership: What's at Stake?

Positive psychology researchers completed a "meta-analysis," a study of nearly every scientific happiness research article available. In this study, they reviewed over 200 studies on 275,000 people around the world.[5] Their findings prove that happiness leads to success in your work, health, relationships, sociability, creativity, and energy.

Your Life

What if you continue to live your life without true inner happiness and contentment? What if you do not reach your full potential as a human being?

Being consistently unhappy for long periods of time negatively affects a person in countless ways. It weakens the immune system, causes sleep and digestive problems, affects personal relationships, and leaves behind a feeling of unfulfillment. It causes low self-esteem and hinders one from reaching his full potential. When a person is not happy, they experience regret and cannot inspire others. They cannot be a role model for their family, children, or friends. They will feel stuck, trapped, and both angry and sad that they are not living the life that they want.

Physical Health

When continuous stress goes unchecked for long time periods, the outcomes are extremely damaging. This damage occurs when you face challenges without relief or relaxation between said challenges. Chronic stress leads to physical symptoms, including headaches, elevated blood pressure, upset stomach, and muscle and chest pain and can potentially invoke anxiety and affect your motivation. Sustained stress leads to more permanent changes in the brain's regulating behavior resulting in over- or undereating, social withdrawing, or exercising less. It can become really harmful when substances like drugs or alcohol are used to self-medicate, which keeps the body in a stressed state and creates more problems. Prolonged stress can affect employment and productivity, as well as a person's reputation. Stress makes it difficult to recognize painful emotions and can affect romantic relationships. When a person is extremely stressed, she usually will mistreat those closest to her. Stress can also cause weight gain and age one's physical appearance.

Our knowledge about stress is as important as the quantity and type of stress present in our lives. We have the ability to reframe stressful events and see them as challenges and, in doing so, can lower its negative physical and psychological effects. Studies have shown that there's an increased risk of death when people experience high stress levels and believe that said stress is really bad for them.[6] Human connection aids in building resilience to buffer the effects of stress. In addition to changing our beliefs about stress, helping others; spending time in nature; listening to natural sounds such as birds chirping, water flowing in a creek, or the sound of waves lapping on a beach; eating three to seven servings of vegetables and fruit daily; and deep rhythmic breathing can relieve stress.

Life has tremendous gifts to offer you if you slow down to enjoy them. These gifts include the close connection you have with people in your life, the wonders of nature, daily experiences such as waking up to watch the sun rise, accomplishing purposeful goals and work, and knowing that all humans, animals, and life are intimately connected. Such gifts can be viewed as presence in your life, enabling you to appreciate who you are and what you are experiencing. When you feel fearful, uncertain, and overwhelmed, your perspective narrows. You don't see all the possibilities for yourself or for your career—you literally miss out on daily occurring miracles. With your brain full of thoughts of worry and negativity, it's easy to get lost and not notice what's happening around you.

Positivity, optimism, and happiness build resilience, which is the ability to bounce back after challenges. Inevitably, life always throws challenging events at you. The only constant in life is change. If you do not develop inner strength and processes to overcome difficulties, you'll get knocked down time and time again.

The Importance of Connection

How important are the people you're connected to in your life? Are you a parent, a spouse, a sibling, or a friend? Are your parents and grandparents still alive? Those you care about really want you to be happy. When you are continuously unhappy, you negatively affect their lives and cause them worry. Human energy is an open-loop circuit, meaning that your energy absolutely affects those surrounding you. Every single day, you make a choice about how you want to show up for those you care about.

Your Career

How will your leadership career progress if you do not evolve as a leader? What will be the effects on you if you continue to lead while stressed, frustrated, and overwhelmed?

When you approach life with a negative perspective and don't have the leadership tools necessary, it greatly affects your career. By not changing your outlook and using the tools, you adversely influence work relationships with your direct reports, peers, and bosses. Unhappy and disengaged leaders are less likely to be asked to join new projects and teams. Your overall business success and the success of the business itself are directly impacted by your ability to create strong, positive, and lasting relationships with those with whom you work.

You risk the opportunity of not being promoted and/or achieving your dream career. You jeopardize not increasing your salary, benefits, and freedom to create a better life for yourself, your family, and community. Your position might even be at stake, with the possibility of losing your leadership role altogether. You could absolutely reach a plateau—a financial-earning ceiling—and not create the life for yourself and your family that you desperately desire. You might not be able to support your parents and other loved ones as well.

People do not leave organizations; they leave their boss. You can work extremely hard to recruit strong talent and spend time, money, and effort to train them. However, they won't work with you if you aren't supportive, positive, and engaged with them.

One of the most challenging parts of leadership is losing people from your team to the competition. It's unmotivating to you and negatively shakes up the morale of the remaining team members. When you don't have close relationships with your team members, you'll be blindsided by these resignations. Your boss and stakeholders will demand to know why people are exiting your team. When open positions do exist on your team, it takes extensive energy and work to attract, interview, and hire new employees. This energy and work are taken away from your strategic projects that propel your business forward. It is exhausting! Thus, maintaining strong relationships is extremely important to maintaining a strong and loyal team.

It's very difficult to have a work-life balance when you cannot achieve your targets and goals. As a new leader, I worked around the clock; my life was a blend of sleep and work and not much else. Such continuous long hours take a toll on one's mind, body, and spirit. Long hours spent working impedes spending much-needed time with your friends and family members. This lack of socialization directly decreases your personal happiness, and it becomes a tiring, vicious cycle. In addition, long hours mean less time to prioritize exercise, eating nutritiously, etc.

Work-life balance is an interesting concept and can be very personal. I've spent numerous hours studying the happiest employees in the world and found that the ones with the highest satisfaction do not work around the clock. They have time to play sports, socialize, be outdoors, and have downtime to relax. While working long hours may be glorified in many developed countries, it isn't a recipe for a happy life. In the most extreme cases, overwork leads to divorce and strained relationships with one's children. Do you want to work around the clock for the next 5, 10, or 20 years? I spent many years doing just that until I realized that there's a much better way! You can be wildly successful and have a healthy, balanced life, and I will show you how in Chapter 8 and throughout the *Be a Happy Leader* methodology.

Early in my leadership career, I received feedback from more experienced leaders who stated I was perceived as an "Energizer bunny," who was always "running around." It wasn't a compliment and was difficult to hear. Because my team wasn't achieving all the ownership metrics given to us, I worked around the clock and around the company. My work effort was visible, but it hurt my reputation as a leader. Think about it: If you're spending a lot of time at work and still not achieving your goals, your peers and boss likely will think "Wow. What is he/she doing all day/week?" You want to have a very positive reputation. You don't want to be seen by peers and stakeholders as someone who "spins their wheels" monthly and who isn't moving forward quickly. Your reputation in your organization and career is tantamount to your success. Now, there are industries where overwork is absolutely valued, and every person in the organization does it. As a professional and a leader, you are responsible for choosing if you want to join a company that highly values overwork. I honestly believe that the number of hours worked weekly do not equal career success. It's what you accomplish with those hours that really matters.

Your Organization

How happy are the directors and managers whom you lead? How much money is your company losing due to the unhappiness of your leaders and teams? Monumental financial impact occurs in an organization when its managers are not engaged. According to a Gallup poll, managers have the greatest impact on employee engagement. Only 35% of American managers are engaged at work, while 51% aren't engaged, and 14% are actively disengaged.[7]

The "not engaged" group costs the United States between $77 billion and $96 billion annually through the impact on those they manage. Each manager's job is to engage with their employees daily, and Gallup research demonstrates that the majority of managers today are perceived as "checked out."

If you don't motivate and inspire your team, their work suffers. If they don't feel connected to their direct reports and peers and to their work, it's guaranteed that they'll be less productive. They'll not enjoy working and likely will procrastinate and then rush through the work with less accuracy and care. If your team members feel negative about their work, they are less creative and open-minded. Happy employees and productivity are intertwined, and in today's competitive environment, leaders and organizations cannot afford to have wasted time and lower productivity. A team at the University of Oxford's Saïd Business School completed a study that evidenced exactly this: Happier people do a better job.[8] The six-month study of 1,800 call-center workers at the British telecom firm BT found a clear causal effect of happiness on productivity. The workers were asked to rate their happiness each week via an email survey comprised of five emoji buttons ranging from very sad to very happy. Happy employees not only worked faster, making more calls per hour, but they also achieved 13% higher sales than their unhappy colleagues.

How important is brand reputation to you and your organization? There is a direct correlation between happy employees, Glassdoor reviews, and satisfied customers.[9] The most successful companies around the globe are customer obsessed. Is there room for improvement in your company's customer satisfaction right now? When you review all the employees who directly care for customers, how positive and effective are their managers and leaders? It does not take much to bruise a brand's reputation. The majority of the time, it stems from an action made by a displeased employee. One adverse comment or action can usher the negative behavior to digital status, where it then can go viral. The more exposure a negative event gets, the worse it can be for the brand's reputation. One example of this is when musician Dave Carroll flew with United Airlines and his $3,500 guitar arrived in pieces. He raised the issue with the airline employees who "showed complete indifference." When he tried to file a claim for compensation, they told him he was ineligible because the claim hadn't been filed within 24 hours. Carroll spent nearly nine months trying to get compensation and wrote a protest song. The song, "United Breaks Guitars," has its own music video with over 20 million views on YouTube. United's stock valuation went into a short-term free fall, and the incident has not been forgotten.

Happy Sales Professionals

As you know, my background is in sales and marketing. I personally sold to customers and led sales professionals for 14 years. Sales professionals successfully sell more and build stronger relationships with their customers when they are happy. Harvard's Shawn Achor has proven through over a decade of research that happiness can increase sales by up to 37 percent! After spending 12 years at Harvard University, Achor has become one of the world's leading experts on the connection between happiness and success. His research on mindset made the cover of *Harvard Business Review,* and his TED Talk is one of the most popular of all time with over 23 million views.

Happy salespeople are more loyal and recruiting top salespeople from the competition will be easier. Emotions are contagious and will carry over to your customers, who feel the positive personalities and tones via phone and video calls, email, and social media. Happy salespeople think outside the box and collaborate with each other and other departments in your organization to accomplish their goals.

What If You Stay the Same?

What's at stake if you don't prioritize your personal happiness and experience joy, excitement, and calm in your life? Everything is! We aren't immortal beings. It's a fact of life that on any single day, we can become sick or pass away. I don't want to live my life unhappy and full of regret. Do you?

What's at stake if you don't learn how to harness positivity in your daily life? You risk negatively affecting your career, your health, and your relationships. You might stop dreaming, lower your professional goals, and not be aligned with your purpose. No one wants to disappoint the people they admire, care about, or themselves. You must believe that you can become a happy leader. Proven tools are available and within reach, and I will give you these tools in the following chapters. I want you to feel proud, optimistic, and energized by your future!

Happy Leader Prompts

1. On a scale from 1 to 10, how do you rate yourself in these areas today?
   - Physical Health
   - Personal Relationships
   - Balance
   - Stress
   - Professional Relationships
   - Optimism
   - Professional Career
   - Team

2. On a scale from 1 to 10, how is your team and organization doing in the following areas?
   - Engagement
   - Productivity
   - Sales
   - Customer Satisfaction
   - Brand Reputation
3. In six months from now, where do you want to move the needle for yourself and your team in each of the areas above?

CHAPTER 3:
A Desire for More

I n December during my first semester at university, my life consisted of attending classes, studying, waitressing part time, and spending the majority of my time with friends. We snowboarded on the local mountains, hung out at each other's houses, and went out on the town most nights. We definitely lived for the nightlife and would stay at the dance clubs until closing three to four nights weekly. I partied too often and too hard, and it affected my schoolwork and my job. The high of dancing, meeting new people, and being carefree was the best part of my life at the time.

My First University Experience
One morning, I shot up suddenly in my bed as if electricity were running through me. My stomach dropped as I realized I had missed an important final exam and would receive a D in that class. I had never received a grade lower than a B in my entire life.

I had always been really strong in English, receiving A's or A+'s my entire life. This might not seem like a bad GPA for someone in her first university semester but receiving a D in English was like a massive punch to my gut. My heart sank, and my self-esteem plummeted. I was devastated. The letter grade D ripped a hole through my core. The D in English symbolized my lack of focus, prioritizing of partying, and the feeling of being lost in my life.

I dropped out of college after one semester, thinking, "This is a waste of my time and money." I was extremely embarrassed and disappointed in myself and knew that I had disappointed my parents, grandparents, and the rest of my family. Out of touch with my emotions, I didn't feel grounded at all.

I was lost and unhealthy and had no idea then what I was doing with my life. Really unhappy, I self-medicated by partying way too much. My father had really wanted me to attend college after I graduated high school, so I had chosen a handful of random classes and was "sort of attending." I had always been a great student academically, and even though I partied a lot during high school, I had kept a good balance of partying, sports, and good grades. Now I was living on my own and was out of touch with who I was on the inside.

A month after I dropped out, my best friend and I packed our bags and moved to the next province, Alberta. We chose the city of Calgary because we knew a few people who lived there and because the drinking age in Alberta was 18 versus 19 in our province of British Columbia. Great decision-making, right?

We rented a one-bedroom apartment in a disadvantaged area of the city, and both got hired waitressing at the same restaurant. We shared my bright yellow convertible Geo Tracker. (It was -20°F in the winter in Calgary, and the Tracker's zip-up roof was a joke!) We waitressed five days a week and partied the rest. We could walk from our apartment to a strip of bars and nightclubs, and we went out dancing four to five times a week. We spent all the money we made monthly. It's honestly shocking that neither one of us ever got hurt or landed in serious trouble.

Eventually my friend moved back to our hometown of Kelowna, so I rented an apartment of my own. Located next to a Safeway Grocery Store in downtown Calgary, the tiny studio had one window looking out at a brick wall. At the time, I was dating a 28-year-old waiter who still lived with his parents. My partying and unhealthy lifestyle continued, and I still felt lost and unhappy. My life didn't have a tremendous amount of meaning, the man I was dating wasn't right for me, and I felt disconnected from my family and most of my friends.

Tropical Trips—An Eye-Opener

That winter my mother decided to take my two sisters and me on a two-week trip to Costa Rica with her boyfriend and his two sons. I was beyond excited to get out of the Canadian cold. It was the second time that we'd ever been out of Canada or the United States. (When I was 16, she'd taken us for a week to Puerto Vallarta, Mexico, and I had loved every second of it.) The Costa Rica trip was beyond eye-opening, filled with culture, exploration, and new experiences. I loved how the heat felt on my body and how being in the tropics energized my soul. We traveled around by van to various places and stayed at local hole-in-the-wall motels. We were really traveling, and I thought it was incredible. It was the first time in a long time that I felt happy, energized, and alive on the inside. As I lay down in the warm sun, I felt introspective, and a big question kept popping up in my mind: What did I want to do with my life?

I returned to freezing Calgary, my tiny ugly apartment, my uninspiring job, and my 28-year-old boyfriend. It was such a drastic change from the Central American country that I'd just spent two weeks in. I was disappointed in myself and the life I was creating. The Costa Rica trip had expanded my horizons, which had contracted as soon as I returned home. My freezing, unpleasant, and unhealthy life felt black and white compared to the vibrant, colorful way I felt in the tropics. In Calgary, I felt small, unimportant, and without direction. When I was in Costa Rica, I felt motivated, inquisitive, and optimistic about new possibilities for my life.

A few months after returning to Calgary, my boyfriend recklessly crashed my yellow GEO Tracker. It was a warm spring day, and we had spent it rafting down a river with friends. We were still in our swimsuits as the two of us climbed into the small vehicle. My boyfriend hopped into the driver seat and cranked up the music really loud. My friend and her boyfriend were in a smaller car in front of us, which we followed up a narrow dirt road. A dirt embankment was located on one side, and a steep one dropped down the other side into the river that we'd just left.

Suddenly, my boyfriend floored the gas pedal and attempted to pass my friend's car. I grasped the handle in front of my seat, screaming, "What are you doing? Stop! Stop!" He didn't listen. We were right next to their car on the narrow road, my fists were white, and my heart was pounding. Slamming into the dirt bank, my Tracker rolled and flipped over in the blink of an eye. When we landed, I was upside down in my seat, with a giant piece of roof metal jutting dangerously close to my face. My boyfriend was bleeding and attempting to exit his seat. I slowly undid my seat belt and maneuvered myself out of the vehicle. He got out as well, and, though bloody, wasn't seriously hurt. I took a few steps away from the car and looked at the crunched vehicle my father and I had picked out together on my 16th birthday. The car was totaled, yet I didn't have a scratch on my body. I glared at my boyfriend angrily and thought, "What am I doing with this loser? What am I doing with my life?"

I again had disappointed my parents, my friends, and myself, and now I was also car-less. I was so embarrassed.

It was a very painful point in my life, and definitely one of my lows. The wreck was also one of the biggest gifts that I have ever received. The accident forced me to take a good, hard look in the mirror and ask myself, "Who am I, and what do I want to do with my life?"

Afterwards, my boyfriend and I broke up, and I began to ease up on the partying. I remember one of my older friends at the time asking me, "Don't you want to go back to school, Tia? Do you really want to be a waitress for the next 10 years?"

He took me on the train in the northern part of the city to the University of Calgary to walk around the campus. It was calming, spacious, and felt so different from my downtown life. As a result, I decided to sign up for classes and to start working towards a business degree.

My Summer Epiphany

One cold January morning, I was sitting on the floor of my studio apartment and thinking to myself, "I want to go back to the heat; I want to go somewhere sunny and tropical." I have no idea why, but right then and there I decided that I would go work on a cruise ship that summer. I would waitress and have the opportunity to travel in the sun. I started researching the cruise lines that went to Mexico and the Caribbean. As I was researching, a pop-up window appeared on my computer screen: "Summer Internships on Hilton

Head Island, South Carolina." It had a beautiful photo of a harbor with boats and palm trees and looked incredible. I clicked on it, read all about the opportunities, and applied. Shortly thereafter, I had a phone interview with a company that ran a children's summer camp, and they offered me an internship position. I was so excited when I told my family.

I spent three glorious months on this gorgeous island taking care of elementary-aged kids, making new friends from all over the United States, and basking in the hot, humid South Carolina sun. I was in heaven. I felt like the "real" Tia. The Tia hidden deep down inside me. The Tia who would sing, laugh, skip, and smile all the time. My inner happy child let me know that she was still in there.

This experience enabled me to learn about an industry centered on tourism. I spent time at huge Marriott resorts where I met families from all over. Every Friday, my company would go sailing on this gorgeous boat, and pods of bottlenose dolphins would swim next to us. All the students who lived in the internship condo building with me worked for various companies located all over the island. I learned there was a business of travel, and I wanted to be a part of it. That summer, I had an epiphany: "I want more! I am more! I can do more!"

Major Life Change

After I returned to Calgary, Alberta, I began waitressing again and took the train to the University of Calgary to study. I felt happier than before I left but certainly not at the level of happiness I felt when I was living in South Carolina. I realized that I had to leave freezing cold Calgary and Canada, so I decided to move to the United States.

I visited University of Calgary's study-abroad center to research American universities. One book I reviewed discussed schools with degrees in tourism and hospitality. I read a list of five or so and became very excited when I saw the possibilities: University of Denver, University of San Diego, Cornell, and—the University of Hawaii. (Remember, I'm from Northern British Columbia, Canada. I grew up in a log cabin on a street with eight other log cabins, and that was the sum total of our "town.") I held the book to my chest thinking, "Yes, University of Hawaii!"

That night, I applied to their Travel Industry Management School in Honolulu, Oahu, located in the valley behind Waikiki Beach. Three weeks later, I heard from the school and set up a time to speak with admission officials. Although I was an international student, they were willing to lower the tuition due to my American citizenship. A few weeks later, I received a large envelope in the mail containing my acceptance letter.

I called my father with the news from the floor of my ugly, depressing, dark studio apartment. I told him I had applied and been accepted and that I wanted to transfer schools in the following August. My mother's eldest brother had lived in Honolulu for decades, so I would also have family there as well. We discussed how we could possibly make it work with financial scholarships, me working, and his support. After some time and discussion, my father said I could go. I was moving to Hawaii! I felt motivated and that my life finally had a purpose.

Welcome to America!

On a warm August morning, I woke up on the island of Oahu. I had arrived late the night before and had seen only a bit of the city on my ride from the airport to the college dorm building on campus. My roommate hadn't yet arrived, so I was alone in our small tower dorm room. I sat up in my small bed, smiled, and ran to the window. I could see past the campus, over the skyscrapers of Waikiki, and out to the ocean. Adrenaline shot through my body, and I screamed out loud. I quickly dressed and grabbed my tiny backpack, throwing in a towel, map, sunscreen, my wallet, and water.

I started to explore the campus and the city in the warm, humid Hawaiian sunshine. The city smelled of tropical flowers mixed in with city scents. People were busy going about their day, the streets were filled with cars, and I felt as if I were walking on the lightest cloud. I crossed the concrete bridge over the Ala Wai Canal and entered Waikiki. The tall hotels and apartment buildings were shiny, looming, and glorious. I kept walking and didn't stop until I reached the glistening, warm yellow sands of Waikiki beach.

I spread out my soft towel on the beach and threw down my backpack. I still had not turned around to look back to where I had come from. Goose bumps covered my skin, and the sun's rays held my body and hugged my soul. The buzzing of tourists talking, playing, and walking was the best sound that I'd ever heard in my life. I walked into the warm turquoise ocean water, and when it was deep enough, I began swimming. I swam, and I swam, and I swam, yet I did not look back. I kept swimming through the bath-like angelic waters for what felt like forever. Then, I slowly turned around and took my first look back at Oahu. It was bright green, mountainous, and reminded me of the fictional island to which Peter Pan flew with Wendy. To my right was the Diamond Head volcano, which majestically shot up into the soft blue sky. Streams of neighborhoods flowed down each ridge of the lush mountains. The city of Honolulu loomed large and spread out along the entire island side. Waikiki Beach was a beautiful golden ribbon, and the Waikiki skyline looked just like a postcard. I could hear the sound of the waves crashing next to me and people laughing as they surfed the waves on boards and in traditional Hawaiian canoes. The warm water that I was treading held all of me. My mouth had the taste of tropical salty water. Big joyful tears rolled down my face. Authentic happiness and true contentment filled every single inch of my body, mind, and soul. I was so proud of myself. I was so grateful. I was in awe. I had made this happen. I was living in Hawaii!

You might be thinking, well, of course she's happy, she moved to a tropical island. Yes, the environment and climate contributed to my emotional state, but so much more was happening. Prior to moving to Honolulu, I had felt that my life hadn't had much meaning. I hadn't connected to what I was doing or why I was doing it. When you have meaningful, concordant goals that you are working towards, the journey itself towards those goals increases your happiness. Yes, achieving the goals is important, but you're more satisfied during the days and the present moments you experience when you're on the path to achievement.

In addition, my psychology had been affected by loneliness, stress, and drinking alcohol. My mental health was also affected by the type of foods that I had been eating and my not getting consistent healthy sleep. In Calgary, I had started to learn and grow by going back to university, but what I was studying was not aligned with my passions and interests. I was learning, but what I was learning didn't excite me.

As previously mentioned, the number one predictor of human happiness is human connection—spending time with people that you really care about. While I had a few great friends in Calgary, I hadn't spent enough time with them. When we did spend time together, we would go out for dinner, drinks, and dancing. Healthy relationships come from spending time together, connecting during healthy activities, really getting to know each other, and being open and honest with each other. My emotional state had been merely mediocre in Calgary. In Hawaii, tons of opportunity existed for me to increase all of the pleasant emotions such as excitement, serenity, and amusement.

My Education Begins

School began, and I became completely engaged and motivated to excel. The classes were fascinating and interactive. New friendships blossomed and grew, and incredible mentors who inspired me entered my life. I worked in restaurants and completed several travel internships as part of the tourism program. The most intense and eye-opening was an internship with the complex director of sales and marketing for the four Starwood Hotels Waikiki.

On a personal happiness scale, I was really happy. Not only had I moved to islands in the middle of the Pacific Ocean, but I had discovered my passion and had aligned myself with the travel and hospitality industries. Those industries were extremely interesting to me, and I grew as a person. When your brain is learning, positive emotions occur, and you feel happier.

As a child, I had always been really interested in school, participated in class, and even spent time teaching the children needing assistance. It was in Hawaii that I became that person again, the real me. I now had a future path for both my personal life and for my career, which was clear and exciting for me. Life held a huge amount of purpose and meaning for me to wake up to every single day. For the first time in my entire life, I was connected to my future self. I clearly could see the vision of a great career and a fulfilling personal life.

My physical health was strong in Hawaii, which also directly contributed to how happy and well I felt psychologically and emotionally. I ate healthily, exercised regularly, and with my new friends, stretched and practiced yoga, and finally was getting enough sleep. My friendships and relationships flourished as I lived authentically, and the energy I gave off was infectious. Because I was aligned with my passions, I met people with similar passions at the University of Hawaii. These relationships were not solely based on having a great social life, and they increased my pleasant emotions and contributed to my happiness.

Looking back, with all that I know about positive psychology, many reasons existed as to why my happiness shot up with this move. The number one predictor of happiness is human connection. I had that with my family and friends in Hawaii. Its natural beauty, my outdoor experiences, and my tourism studies gave me meaning, and I was in awe almost daily. In addition, I was learning, which contributed to my intellectual well-being, and I exercised regularly and ate healthier, all proven to make one feel happier. My tourism program also taught me how to be a successful leader, and my mentors and internships provided me with strong, inspiring examples of positive and effective leadership.

Post-Graduation

After graduation, I was accepted into the Starwood Management Training Program in Waikiki, and I spent time in San Francisco working at the Palace Hotel. At the end of the training program, I moved into a complex sales role in Waikiki, and I was very excited about starting a real career. I became a leader at a young age and had an incredible career selling and marketing hotels in the United States and in Turkey. I found my purpose and meaning from working in teams, leading others, and driving businesses forward.

Do you want to better your life? To feel more fulfilled, energized, and that you have a purpose? Deep down, do you know that you were made for more? Do you want to make a change, but you don't know where and how to start? Do you want to be happier and really make a difference as a positive, inspirational leader?

I have traveled through many ups and downs in life. After moving to Honolulu, Hawaii, and rediscovering my joy and passion for life and work, I promised myself to never settle in my career or my personal life. You, too, can absolutely desire more and chase after your big, bold dreams. Read onward, as I am going to show you how to continuously make shifts and adjustments in your life to become happier and thrive!

Happy Leader Prompts

1. Reflection Exercise: What are the two to three experiences that you have had in your life that have taught you the biggest lessons? What happened and what did you learn?
2. Journaling Activity: Where do you want to grow and expand personally and professionally?
3. Who are your mentors and coaches in your life today? Who are you currently mentoring and coaching?

CHAPTER 4:
The Possibility

What desires do you have for your life and your career right now? When I started working as a director at the age of 26, I wanted to be personally happy and fulfilled, make a positive impact on the people that I was leading, and do well professionally so that I could grow in my career and live and work in many different places. Marriage and children were part of my future plan, and I knew that I always wanted to be passionate and excited about what I was doing for work. I wanted to make a difference.

Put to the Test
I was the director of sales and marketing at the London West Hollywood at Beverly Hills Hotel. I led a team of 15 talented individuals, was on the executive committee, and was tasked with generating over $50 million annually between room revenue and

food and beverage. It was a fast-paced career, and in sales, you are only as good as your last month. Stress has always been a very common factor throughout my career, and this position was no different.

After giving birth to each of my daughters, I went back to work after a mere 12 weeks. In my opinion, that's way too soon for a mother. Three months after having a baby, a mother is still exhausted and must wake up multiple times nightly for extended time periods. She's still getting used to what it is like to be a parent and learning how to take care of her new baby. Also, three months is right when a baby's personality begins to show, and they become interactive. However, I've always been a career-focused individual, and I've always had motivation, ambition, and a work ethic. I realize now, looking back, that I absolutely should have had more time to bond with my babies, heal, and gain more strength both psychologically and emotionally.

When I returned to work after having my second daughter, I attempted to balance having my executive leadership career; being a mom, wife, and friend; staying healthy; and fulfilling all the personal expectations I had for myself. Nowadays, I tell people that I am a recovering perfectionist.

At that time, I was really attempting to be as perfect as possible in all areas. That desire to be perfect throughout my life stemmed from being the oldest of three children, my constant desire to please people, and an identity intimately connected to achievement. My perfectionism began in my early 20s when I moved to Honolulu and stayed with me until my late 30s.

I felt as if I were failing. I had a two-year-old and a three-month-old, and I was drained both physically and emotionally. Everything that I thought I knew about myself, my identity, my strengths, my life, felt upended.

One night, after I had just finished putting our toddler and baby to sleep, I collapsed on the couch. Every ounce of my body, mind, and soul was exhausted. I had been up four times the night before with the baby and had woken up at 6 A.M. to get ready for work. I had spent the morning with the girls, worked a full day at my stressful job, rushed home to have dinner with the girls and attempted to squeeze in some playtime, and finally juggled giving them a bath, reading them books, and putting them to sleep. It was extremely difficult to be present when I was with my girls after a long workday, as my mind was still racing from the day.

My husband walked in the door a few minutes later. He came over to the dark living room area and said, "Hi, my love. How was your day?" I looked at him and began bawling uncontrollably. He dropped his gray backpack on the floor and walked over to me with open arms to give me a hug. I stood up, pushed away his extended arms, and walked around the glass coffee table to face him.

"My day? My day was horrible! I'm so tired, and I'm failing. I'm not doing a great job at work, I never have time to exercise and take care of myself, I never see my friends anymore, and I'm failing as a mom to our girls."

"Oh, honey, you are doing great. You are just really tired right now."

"I am *not* just really tired!" I screamed at him. Tears streamed down my face and fell on my expensive teal work dress. I hadn't even taken the time to change into comfortable clothes after work.

"I'm not doing any of this right, and I'm not enjoying any of it! I'm a lot more than tired."

He walked over to me as I stood in the middle of the carpet sobbing, head down, and shoulders collapsed. He placed his big, warm arms around me and held me. I cried for what felt like forever.

"Maybe you should call someone, Tia. You could call your mom or your sisters and get their thoughts on what is going on."

"Yeah. Okay. I will call someone."

I walked through the dark apartment to our bedroom, changed, and collapsed into bed. My eyes were swollen from all the tears. My mind raced with negative and self-critical thoughts. It took me a long time to fall asleep that night, and I knew the next day was going to be another rough day.

The next morning, on my short drive to work, I called my friend Galit, whom I'd worked with at the W Hotels of New York. We'd both moved to NYC at the same time in 2008 and had walked to work together multiple times a week. Galit knew pre-mom Tia and was a close friend.

"Hey, Tia! What's going on? How are you?"

"Hi, Galit." She could hear that I was crying. "I'm failing. I'm failing at being a mom. I'm failing at the hotel. I'm a horrible wife and friend."

"Oh, Tia, you are not failing at anything. You're a new mom! I think you should call Cherie Healey, my amazing life coach."

"What's a life coach?"

"Just call her. I'm going to send you her number right now. Call her today."

Can you relate to my feelings of imbalance and lack of fulfillment? What are you going through right now? I suggest you follow my example and seek out some answers.

I ended up reaching out to Galit's life coach, Cherie, that day. We had an hour conversation the day after. For the first time in a very long time, I felt real hope after that call. I decided to partner with Cherie for six months. I thought I was hiring her to help me find balance and more spirituality and to create a stronger connection with my husband. At least, that's what I told her that

I needed, and what I thought I needed. A lesson that I learned from her, and one that I want you to remember, is that you are *never* alone. When you are challenged and overwhelmed with your leadership career and in your life, people will always be there to support you. We aren't born resilient; it's a cultivated trait. Resilience is about bouncing back, and it is growing through strategies and healthy habits. I grew from my experience because I hired a life coach. You can always get stronger and wiser, actually; it's what life is all about.

On our very first coaching call, I shared with Cherie that I'd always had an idea of creating a happiness company to help other people become happier. However, I was at a very low point in my life and wasn't sure that I was the right person anymore. Yet, for whatever reason, that thought came out of my mouth. I had always been positive, energetic, and optimistic. And I was deathly afraid that I would never be that person once again.

Cherie grabbed on to my idea of creating a happiness company, and from the beginning of our relationship, we started exploring, creating, and putting pen to paper on what this company could become. I had a large deck to which I would add information and concepts. I became obsessed with learning and understanding what makes people happy. I watched TED Talks and read books and articles about it, and it was then that I discovered that there was something called a "science of happiness" and Martin Seligman's idea that psychologists should start studying really happy people. I remember thinking that I had been one of those really happy people for the majority of my life.

After a couple of months of working with Cherie, I thought, "I can become a coach." By then, I had coached sales professionals for fourteen years. I began by taking life and leadership coaching courses over the phone. I would leave work, hop on calls, and sit in my car outside my apartment building to learn and study. I loved what I was learning.

Birth of the Happiness Workshops

Cherie inspired me to create a happiness workshop. I hired an events experience engineer to create one, and I lead my first workshop at my friend's self-discovery studio in Playa del Rey, a beachside community in Los Angeles. I invited 40 friends and colleagues to join me and held it for free. It was a two-and-a-half-hour experience, and my friend Jeffrey led a yoga session as part of it. I had worked on my "Walking on Sunshine" happiness workshop for months, and I was very nervous to lead it. I also created an attendee survey to be taken afterwards so that I could receive feedback about their experiences. In my workshop, I integrated positive psychology teachings and pair and group exercises and then ended it with a meditation on the beach. It was amazing! I received incredibly positive feedback. I remember thinking, "This is a happiness product that I could sell." I started selling tickets and led several workshops over the next year. When I sold my first corporate workshop to a public relations firm, I was full of excitement and joy.

My company Arrive At Happy, helps businesses drive growth through a culture of engagement and happiness. It incorporates positive psychology, neuroscience, teamwork, trust, and employee happiness into a leadership program. Leadership and employee happiness leads to increased productivity, engagement, sales, teamwork, and innovation. Happy employees positively affect their family and friends. Those happy people then are more generous to their social circles and communities. Arrive At Happy exists so that people can become happier at work and in life and, in turn, make other people happier, leading to more success all around!

My company supports organizations with keynote talks, executive retreats, corporate training, and consulting.

What does my title, "Inspirationist," mean? To me, it means someone who inspires people (and the rest of the world) to dream, live, and connect to who they really are. My company's intention is to inspire organizations, leaders, and people to prioritize their happiness as they travel the path to unlimited success and fulfillment. Wherever you are in your professional career and in your life, there's always an opportunity to be inspired. I chose this professional title because we're all on a happiness journey, and I want to share the secrets and strategies that I know and have studied along the way. My goal is for everyone to truly believe that they are never stuck and that possibilities do exist.

The Annual World Happiness Summit

As I researched the science of happiness online, I discovered that an Annual World Happiness Summit at the University of Miami was scheduled, so I purchased a ticket to attend. I also signed up to be a "tribe coach" to support a group of attendees throughout the weekend. A tribe coach is a certified leadership and life coach who is trained to facilitate attendee connection, learnings, and integration of the summit material. The three-day conference absolutely blew me away! I learned from leading experts about all aspects of personal happiness and what makes humans thrive and connected with the CEO, Karen Guggenheim. The summit's speakers talked about the dark and bright sides of life, filling the 2,000 people in the room with hope and inspiration. I discovered that a happiness professor from Harvard was beginning a new yearlong course where people could receive multiple certifications. I had met people from all over the world and felt that I was in the exact place that I was supposed to be. At the following World Happiness Summit, I was a speaker and shared my story of how the World Happiness Summit had supported me in growing my company.

The Transformational Speaking Retreat

The coach I had worked with, Cherie, recommended that I attend a four-day Transformational Speaking Retreat in Santa Fe, New Mexico. It was there that I found the clarity and confidence to tell my authentic stories. After reflecting back on all my life experiences, I understood why being happy and prioritizing happiness were so important to me. Those who attended this retreat with me were incredible and on similar journeys of sharing their voices. I was moved by their vulnerability.

Your authentic self is inside of you. When you are connected to who you *truly* are, you become the leader you are meant to be. At times, we all feel unsure of ourselves, and I have even felt "imposter syndrome" along the way. Imposter syndrome is the idea that you've only succeeded due to luck and not because of your talent or qualifications. All of us need a peer support system encouraging us to achieve our leadership goals and life dreams. It's wonderful that resources abound to support self-discovery and growth. If you're called to lead people in this life, you'll inevitably stumble upon challenges along the way. Persevere and do not lose the fire that's inside of you!

Positive Psychology Courses

Dr. Ben-Shahar's positive psychology courses were perfect for my journey, and I studied with him for six hours a week for a year. I studied weekly while still holding my position as director of sales and marketing at the London West Hollywood Hotel. I cared for my kids, worked my nine-to-five job, and studied after I put my girls to sleep at night. If you had told me that I would've had enough energy to do my real job and study and create a business on the side, I would've thought you were crazy. The amazing fact is that I was energized from working on the new projects and from learning again. I was motivated by the possibility of being an entrepreneur and the impact that I could have on the world.

As part of my newly created company, Arrive At Happy, I decided to sell and lead happiness retreats. Such a retreat was held on a spring weekend at the Calamigos Ranch in Malibu, California. I created, marketed, and sold tickets for this weekend-long experience. I hired a publicist to support me in obtaining press coverage prior to the retreat and to get journalists to attend and write about the experience. This retreat included healthy food; yoga; breath work; a speaker on the Blue Zones; and group, pair, and individual experiences related to the science of happiness. The weekend was one of the most special experiences of my life to date, and again I was given the confidence to sell my retreats to corporations. I received glowing feedback from each and every one of the retreat's 18 attendees, and lengthy write-ups were published in both *Forbes* and *Yoga Journal*.

Time for a Change

Due to the traction I was gaining with my company and my desperate need to have more time with my young children, I made the decision to request that I move from a full-time to a part-time position at the hotel. At the time, I was coaching several people one-on-one and selling corporate workshops and retreats. I knew that there were places where my husband and I could cut expenses to make it work. I was honestly shocked when my company allowed me to take a pay cut and to continue working part time, but I'd built an incredibly talented sales team, and the numbers were there to support such a change. I now had time to continue to build Arrive At Happy and to spend more time with my family.

Throughout the entire process, there were still many times when I struggled emotionally. Yes, I was motivated by and excited about Arrive At Happy, but I continued to have stressful, challenging days, sometimes weeks, when I was feeling guilty, sad, angry, frustrated, overwhelmed, and anxious, to name a few. I believe that no matter what you're doing, attempting to balance a career and family is challenging. However, I knew that I was moving in the right direction for my family and that I was becoming more self-aware in the process. I was rediscovering who I had always been and, in turn, who I had actually become.

Eventually, I left my corporate position to run my company full time. It was the right decision for me and my family. As I am a huge extrovert, I did miss the camaraderie of working in a large organization and being in and leading teams. However, I was, and am still, very thankful for the flexibility of being my own boss and having more time for my children. I know this is the right path for me for now.

I was filled with pride and gratitude when I was hired to lead a full-day retreat for a global wellness team in the Sacred Valley region in Peru. I had the opportunity to visit Machu Picchu, explore the Sacred Valley, connect with incredible people, and lead a group through a transformational day of self-discovery and happiness. It felt like my heart and soul were bursting at the seams with joy, and I thanked the higher power for this weeklong Arrive At Happy experience!

Certified Chief Happiness Officer

In Copenhagen, Denmark, I became a certified chief happiness officer for happiness at work. The amount of people who say they are "really happy" while working is significantly higher in Denmark than it is in the United States. I followed the results of the Annual World Happiness Report and was intrigued by the happy Scandinavian countries. A Danish company, Woohoo inc., had performed global corporate happiness work for over 18 years, and I learned evidence-based strategies and tactics that leaders can employ to increase the happiness of their employees from Woohoo inc. Happier employees are more productive, engaged, loyal, creative, sell more, and are more collaborative. The list of benefits is tremendous, so I added this new knowledge into my products.

Furthering My Mission

The desire to start speaking onstage and communicating to larger audiences about my mission and knowledge grew inside of me. I became very involved with the National Speakers Association in Los Angeles, taking part in its nine-month Academy membership program and becoming a board member. I was then hired to give keynote talks to both association and corporate audiences. In fact, my podcast, *The Arrive At Happy Leaders Show,* still continues to inspire and motivate leaders to transform their organizations from the inside out.

I spent the first 14 years of my leadership career in the corporate world. Its leaders have the opportunity to impact large groups of people throughout their careers. Part of my mission is to provide leaders with simple strategies and tangible tools to make the right impact. I have studied positive psychology, leadership well-being, employee happiness, the happiest countries, and neuroscience, and I'll continue to study and expand my knowledge throughout my life. Incredible information abounds about positive leadership, and I believe that every leader must know and act on this information. I was born to do this work, and I possess the multiple talents, traits, and qualities to be a happiness leader and an inspirationist. Everyone has the choice every single day to choose joy. It's a powerful skill that has the ability to change your life forever.

What are you going through right now, and what do you truly desire? My personal and professional experiences and learnings can fast-track you in both your leadership career and your life by implementing the methodology outlined in this book. You can learn tangible ways to apply the concepts and create your happy leader path.

The first time that I discovered what choosing a life full of joy and happiness meant occurred when I was 12 years old. My family was living in Kelowna, and my parents were going through a challenging divorce. They were attempting to finalize child custody and finances and figure out how our family would move forward with two separate households. I was definitely old enough to know exactly what was going on, and my parents were transparent with me. I was crushed that our family of five was splitting apart. I tried to protect my two younger sisters from the divorce roller coaster and attempted to find normalcy in our new normal.

My father had always been a very happy-go-lucky person. He also had a thriving social life, and we were always surrounded by friends and family. The divorce definitely took a huge toll on both of my parents, and I realized that the light inside my dad was fading. He was stressed, uncertain, and attempting to learn how to take care of three young girls on his own.

One morning I came downstairs at my dad's house, and his energy was different, lighter. He was playing "I Can See Clearly Now" by Johnny Nash, and the kitchen smelled like fresh bacon and fresh-squeezed orange juice. He was dancing around the room with a big smile on his face.

"Good morning, Dad!"

"Good morning, Tia!"

"Wow, Dad, you seem ... different. Happy birthday! Are you happy because it is your birthday?"

"You know, Tia, I woke up this morning, and I thought to myself, I've had 40 great years and 3 lousy years. It's my birthday, and I don't want to have another bad year. I want to have a great year, and the only person who can make it great is me."

I walked over to him, and we hugged. Small tears ran down my face.

My dad was "back." His circumstances and the events in his world had not changed, but he had made a choice. My parents had gone through a divorce, and to him he had the chance to start fresh. He had reflected back on the 40 good years and made a conscious decision to create a new good year. He wanted to be positive about life, not negative. He chose to look forward and not to look backward. My father used his past great life experiences to get back on track again. He also used the emotion of gratitude, and to this day he says, "Some people say the glass is half empty, and others say it is half full. My overall attitude is I'm just happy to have the glass." He also believes that to be happy in life, less is more. The simple life is where you find the joys in life.

You can choose joy, too! You can put your happiness first. This book can empower and inspire you to make positive choices in your career and in your personal life. I know this is possible because I have seen it happen time and time again. You have everything you need in your hands right now.

Happy Leader Prompts

1. Journaling Exercise: What is your professional mission? What impact do you want to make on the world with your work?

2. Write the word JOY at the top of a piece of paper and write down every single thought that comes to mind when you think of this word.

3. On a scale from 1 to 10, how would you rate your life in the following areas today and where do you want to be six months from now?
   - Career
   - Friends and Family
   - Physical Environment
   - Personal and Spiritual Development
   - Social and Fun
   - Finances
   - Health and Self-Care

CHAPTER 5:

Be A Happy Leader Methodology

At 26 years old, I had just been promoted to director of sales and marketing for the Sheraton Kauai Resort. I had been living in Honolulu for five years and was living now on the south shore of Kauai. It was a huge difference from the hustle of a big city. My small apartment was situated in Lawai Valley and looked out onto a banana tree farm. The entire island had only 46,000 residents and a handful of stoplights. It was quiet, peaceful, and naturally breathtaking. The *Jurassic Park* movies were filmed on the island, and it felt as if I were living back in time.

My First Director Role

My boss, the resort's general manager, had been my mentor years prior in Waikiki. She was successful, driven, and extremely intelligent. Fresh out of the 18-month-long Management Training Program, I was the director leading a sales team of five.

In addition, I was responsible for all the marketing and public relations for the resort. I had a beautiful corner office with windows overlooking a garden and swaying palms. I felt excited, honored, nervous, uncertain, and determined, all at the same time. Many people in the Starwood Waikiki organization questioned why an inexperienced 26-year-old was now running the resort's sales team. To be honest, I was also questioning how I had been hired for the job. Both my direct boss and mentor had 25-year careers in hotel sales, in addition to hotel management and general manager roles. I was hired for the role because my boss and the regional team believed in my ability to learn what I didn't know. The regional vice president and I had spent a lot of time together, and he had seen my leadership potential. I also had proven my work ethic, passion, and drive during my internship with my boss, who believed that I could lead others. I knew that she trusted me and wanted me to succeed, and I was determined to not let her or myself down. I wanted to prove to everyone that I could succeed in the role.

Three months in I had completed my onboarding orientation portion and was responsible for leading my team. I arrived at my office by 8 A.M. and stayed until 8 P.M. or later every day. One of my direct reports, who was a lot older than me, had applied for the director position; she wasn't at all pleased when I landed the role. I consistently made first-time leader mistakes, and absolutely felt like a fish out of water on multiple occasions.

I recall being called into my boss's enormous office for direct feedback. The sunlight streamed through the window, and I could see guests arriving under the Porte cochere and the bellman welcoming them. Air conditioning pumped throughout the office, giving me goose bumps as I sat there in my skirt and blazer suit. The room smelled of fresh tropical flowers and newly brewed coffee. My notebook and pen were in my lap. I could hear my team members and other executive committee members arriving to begin their workday. I knew that I was going to receive my performance feedback, so my heart was beating faster than normal. I had tried my best to assume my new position, but I really didn't know what I didn't know. My boss entered, sat down, looked me directly in the eye, and stated, "Tia, I know that you have been working extremely hard over the past three months getting situated in your new role. Do you feel that you have received adequate training for the position?"

"Yes. Yes, I do."

"How do you feel your team is doing overall?"

"I think they are doing well. We are having our regular meetings and moving forward on all of the key strategies and goals."

"I see ... I have received feedback from Simone that she feels demotivated by the conversations that you are having with her."

My palms started to get sweaty, and my mouth began to feel really dry.

"Oh really? What did she say?"

"She shared that you are asking her a tremendous number of basic questions about her market, her customers, and how to do her job. She feels that you do not know anything about leisure sales, and she doesn't know how you can lead her or teach her anything. Instead of asking her how you can support her and move obstacles out of her way, you're using her to learn about leisure sales. She applied for your position and didn't get it; you did. She must feel that *you* are leading *her*."

Simone was right, I felt.

"Oh my gosh. I apologize. That was certainly not my intention," I replied. Thoughts swirled in my head. How did I get this job in the first place? What am I doing here? How long am I going to last? Does everyone on my team feel this way? Is my boss regretting her decision to promote me? I am way out of my league. This is so embarrassing. I might cry in this office. Don't cry in this office.

"I know. It is understandable that you don't know everything about each person's role on your team. It's imperative that you do not ask your direct reports basic questions that they assume you should know as a director of sales and marketing. You must ask myself and your peers instead of your direct reports if you don't know leisure sales information. Is this clear to you?"

"Yes, absolutely. Thank you for the feedback. I apologize that she feels I'm not leading her properly, and I'll make the necessary changes."

"Great. I need to get ready for our nine o'clock meeting now."

"Of course."

I hurried back to my office down the hall and closed the door. Tears began to well up in my eyes, but I knew that I couldn't allow them to roll down my cheeks as I was due to walk into a meeting with my entire sales team and other managers very soon. Breathing heavily, I had imposter syndrome thoughts swirling around in my head. I wondered how long I could pull the job off. I felt uncomfortable, ashamed, embarrassed, and full of fear. How was I going to survive as a new and very junior leader in this big position?

Uncertainty in Self

Have you ever felt this way? Are there parts of your job and career that are extremely challenging and make you feel very uncomfortable? Imposter syndrome is very common for leaders for a variety of reasons. If you receive negative feedback from a stakeholder, boss, peers, or from direct reports, it's very common for it to affect your psychology and motivation. However, if you've been chosen to be a leader, know that you have passion and drive, and that higher management saw potential in you. Fear is common among leaders—fear of not achieving results, fear of losing great talent, fear of even losing your job. Without the right leadership, support, strategies, and tools, it can be challenging for someone to be a positive force in an organization, and a leadership position can be very challenging to navigate.

At the Sheraton Kauai, I did survive, and I actually learned to thrive. After a year and a half in the position, I was awarded responsibility for two resorts on the island. I opened The Westin Princeville Ocean Resort Villas while still leading the team at the Sheraton, and I spent a total of two and half years on the island. I encountered many challenges that I learned from and grew exponentially. After living in Kauai, I transferred to a leadership position with the five W Hotels in New York City, my dream city at the time. Following New York City, my husband and I transferred to Istanbul, Turkey, for two years to work at the W Istanbul Hotel and then transferred to two different hotels in Los Angeles.

Be A Happy Leader Methodology

I am going to teach you my exact methodology for becoming a happy human, a happy leader, and wildly successful. This book will shed new light on life, happiness, and achieving greatness using my proven *Happy Leader* methodology.

Over the years, I've mentored and coached many people, both inside and outside of sales. Right now, I want you to know that I am your coach, and as such I want you to succeed more than anything. I know you can do it because I did. Going forth, I will continue to share personal stories of where I have been challenged and where I have excelled so you can learn from my mistakes. You don't need to make the same ones I did. You can find your inner joy, be hired for incredible roles where you feel aligned and fulfilled, achieve financial success, and have a ton of fun along the way.

In my last hotel leadership position, I received 98/100 or higher on my annual reviews. I received my full annual bonus, then extra annual bonuses on top of it due to my leadership and performance. You, too, can achieve the very exact same! You can obtain more confidence and greater happiness, in addition to making more money and having a greater impact while succeeding in your role.

Eight Steps to Becoming a Happy Leader

Let's begin your training with an overview of the eight steps in the *Happy Leader* program. Once you've completed and mastered this training, you will understand the key steps to take to reap the benefits in your life and in your career. Here are the eight steps.

Step One—Start with You

Chapter 6, "Step One—Start with You," illustrates how to prioritize your happiness and well-being, find purpose in everyday life, cherish your physical body and mental state, cultivate positive personal relationships, live with awe, and understand the importance of continuous personal development and improvement. After you put all of the personal happiness steps into action, your immune system will be stronger, and you will be healthier and have less stress and anxiety and experience more feelings of joy, calm, and peace. You will be excited and more engaged in your everyday life. Life will be filled with more energy, creativity, and productivity, and consistent daily rituals will be established. Everyone surrounding you will be happier, including your friends, family, coworkers, and team. Your self-confidence will rise, and you will be connected.

Step Two—Zoom Out

Everything in life is about perspective. Chapter 7, "Step Two—Zoom Out," teaches you how to "zoom out" and gain a greater perspective. It details why broadening your view really matters and all the benefits with which it provides you. You learn how to have conscious curiosity in your position and how to continuously raise the bar for yourself, your team, and your whole organization. After you master zooming out, you'll have a stronger connection with your boss, peers, and the stakeholders with whom you work. This perspective provides you with huge professional development and growth. The number of interpersonal challenges you have with other leaders in the organization will be reduced, which will make your work easier and more enjoyable. Then you can execute your goals faster and more accurately and can advance in any organization of which you're a part.

Step Three—Execute Brilliantly

There is, and always will be, a long to-do list and an overflowing email inbox. Step Three, detailed in Chapter 8, "Step Three—Execute Brilliantly," guides you on how to clarify your goals and how to create boundaries. Learn how to recognize success and to become aligned with what is important, in addition to being aware of the benefits of speed, creating plans, and taking action. The chapter provides tips on how to stay organized and gives you a new strategy for learning from people who've already been successful at what you're trying to accomplish. After mastering Step Three, you'll have more time for your health and wellness, personal relationships, relaxation, and personal interests. Your energy, focus, purpose, and confidence will increase. In addition, you will gain a positive reputation in the organization in which you're leading, set a strong example for your peers and team, and have more time to dedicate to them.

Step Four—Prioritize Relationships Over To-Do Lists

Your success is truly defined by the success of the members on your team. Chapter 9, "Step Four—Prioritize Relationships Over To-Do Lists," instructs you on how to prioritize really getting to know your team and the stakeholders who affect both you and your team. Everyone is coachable, so you must learn how to make each person feel valued and appreciated, as acceptance is extremely important to all involved. By placing your newly learned knowledge into practice, your team will feel increased respect, connectedness, cohesiveness, and productivity steeped in a culture of trust, autonomy, team-bonding, and strong work ethic. As a leader, you then can delegate effectively and remain calm when large challenges arise. When stakeholders communicate with you, you won't be personally affronted or waste time working on projects that they don't need. You will know how to make your boss's life easier and how to build a closer relationship with him or her.

Step Five—Your Number One Priority

Are you crystal clear on what your number one priority is as a leader? It's creating a strong team dynamic with your team members. Step Five, covered in Chapter 10, "Step Five—Your Number One Priority," discusses active whole-being listening and consistent and timely communication. I'll share how to give feedback, motivate team members through teaching, and create a positive work environment. No matter what position you have in an organization, if you are a leader, you are a human resource (HR) leader as well. My strategy for fostering a culture of friendship, accountability, and fairness will educate on how to become more self-aware and how to manage yourself during trying circumstances.

Step Six—Measure to Excel

One of my mentors shared the process described in the book *The 4 Disciplines of Execution* with me over a decade ago, and it's one to learn and understand. In Chapter 11, "Step Six—Measure to Excel," you learn how to determine exactly what to measure. Are you clear on your "Wildly Important Goals," and does every team member know them as well? Learn how to inspire people with your goals through transparency, quick meetings, and empowerment. Once this step is mastered, everyone will be aligned and connected with your organization's bigger purpose and goals, and less competition, improved cooperation, clarity, and vision will exist. It's a simple system for everyone that will decrease the numbers of emails you receive.

Step Seven—Be the Spark

You are balancing being an executive and everything else that occurs in your life. You might be an active parent, and/or be looking after other family members, who also needs to prioritize social relationships. Chapter 12, "Step Seven—Be the Spark" discusses how to positively and optimistically lead your team every single day. This chapter dives into your identity, training you how to recognize if your self-view is supportive or harmful. It covers the SPIRE model of well-being and details how you can consistently demonstrate how valuable your entire team is to you. Once this model is set into practice, you can attain calm, balance, and trust within yourself. Your entire team and the organization then become energized; the ripple effects are huge. By becoming the spark, the connection with your team members grows. Your team members, in turn, gain increased positivity and energize each other. As a leader, you learn how to separate yourself from what is happening at work, enabling you to be present in your personal life. Get ready for promotions, new projects, accolades, and financial rewards. Incredibly successful people will want to mentor you, and your success will grow even faster.

Step Eight—Master Your Mindset

How you approach each day in your position is how you approach your career overall. Chapter 13, "Step Eight—Master Your Mindset," illustrates how to master your mindset and to believe in yourself and know your true value. Once your mindset is mastered, your bosses will have tremendous pride in you and want you to remain their employee forever. When challenges arise, you will remain calm and have the ability to move forward with an investigator's approach. This chapter details my Always Yes strategy and how to have a bias towards innovation, possess a clear direction on how to prioritize, and truly enjoy self-development. Professional connections are invaluable, and this chapter illustrates how to approach and foster them. Happiness increases through learning, thus strengthening your résumé as you become a positive leader in your market and industry. Know that you can accomplish anything that you set your mind to!

These eight steps enable you to thrive personally, lead positively, and achieve killer business results! Wouldn't it be fantastic to create job security, a stable future, and positively impact other people in your life? How would your life change if you were truly happy at work and more present at home? What would happen when you consistently achieve your goals and maintain healthy habits?

Successful completion of all eight steps can teach you to be calm, motivated, confident, and inspirational. You will be physically and psychologically healthy. Your immune system will be strong, your personal relationships will flourish, and you'll receive consistent great annual reviews! Become a positive force of change in your organization and truly affect everyone who works for you and with you. It's time to have fun, enjoy your life, and move up the company or industry ladder, or even grow your business successfully!

By positively impacting those you lead and work with, you positively impact their family and friends, including their health and their happiness, transforming the world we live in one team at a time! In the article titled, "Relational Energy at Work: Implications for Job Engagement and Job Performance," found in the *Journal of Applied Psychology*, the three authors reveal that "not only do positively energizing leaders affect their business unit and employee performance, but their influence extends to the family life of employees as well. Employees' families are significantly influenced for the better by positive leaders."[10]

Do you want to live your life going through the motions, or do you want to be present and joyful? Do you want to take charge of your career and your own happiness? I am giving you the leadership playbook and my exact methodology—every single tactic that you need is right here. Let's begin!

Happy Leader Prompts

1. Journaling Exercise: What did you learn from your very first leadership role: what to do and what not to do?
2. Rate yourself from 1–10, with 1 ranking as Poor and 10 being Excellent, on each of the eight Happy Leader steps.

Write down the reason why you rated yourself your score on each one.

3. Who will support you as you grow and develop on your Happy Leader journey?

CHAPTER 6:

Step One—Start with You

Think back to a time in your life when you were feeling excited and happy. Close your eyes right now and envision where you were, who you were with, and what was happening. How old were you? How did you spend your time? What did you see, taste, smell, touch, and hear? Hold those images in your mind, feeling the sensation in your body and soul.

You might have thought of a recent time in your life, or you might have gone back a lot further, maybe even thinking of a childhood memory. Keep thinking of this memory of a really happy time in your life as you read through Step One with me. It's really important that you think about the happiest times in your life, as they are powerful and motivating tools for you. Doing so enables you to understand your capability of being really happy and supports you in creating clear visions of what you need for your future work and life.

Remember the story I told you about the day I moved to Honolulu and of my first walk into the Pacific Ocean in Chapter 3? I can close my eyes and remember this day and period of my life as if it were yesterday—what incredible feelings of pride and pure joy I experienced! I use memories like these as my internal compass. My internal compass is connecting to how I feel physically, emotionally, psychologically, and spiritually. As I progress in my life, I regularly tune in to how I am feeling in all of these areas. I use these peak moments of happiness in my life to assist me in making decisions and staying true to who I am and my values. When I am feeling really "off," and we all know when we are, I think back to those times of inner peace and tell myself, "I need to get back there."

Numerous myths and misconceptions encompass what makes us happy and what happiness even is. Pleasure is often mistaken for lasting happiness. You might feel pleasure when you purchase something, such as a new car, or when you spend money to go on a great vacation. Some people find pleasure in drinking alcohol, shopping, gambling, or watching television. These pleasurable moments are spikes in pleasant emotions, and they make us feel really good. Another misconception is that having money, titles, and success will make you happier. Making more money and career advancement will not necessarily make you happier. However, far too many people rely on money and advancement to bring them the majority of their happiness, and yet it doesn't fulfill them. Another misconception is that a happy life is devoid of pain—that happy people are "happy" all the time. However, there is no such thing. Every single person on earth, even the happy ones, has and feels pain. No one lives a life full of smiles and laughter, a life of being constantly happy. Life's ups and downs happen to all of us.

Different experiences and events give us spikes in pleasure and those feel-good emotions. I'm not here to teach you how to find short-term pleasure. What I want to do is talk to you about your "baseline" of happiness and instruct you on how to increase it. Think about your heart rate right now as you are reading this book. You have a resting heart rate, which is the number of times that your heart beats per minute. Now, if I asked you to put down this book and run back and forth 10 times across the room you're in, your heart rate would elevate. Think of this increased rate as a happiness "pleasure high." While this rate increased, it eventually will drop down again to your resting level.

Now, if you sprinted twice a day, every day, for the next 60 days, did yoga twice a week, and went for long walks weekly, your resting heart rate would change. Your heart rate variability (HRV) is an indicator of your health; it measures the variation in time between each heartbeat. If a person's system is in more of a fight-or-flight mode, the variation between subsequent heartbeats is low. If one is in a more relaxed state, the variation between beats is high. In other words, the faster you are able to switch gears, the more resilience and flexibility. A low HRV is associated with an increased risk of death and cardiovascular disease.

Just like your resting heart rate, you have a resting level of happiness, which is known as your *happiness baseline*. You can choose daily and weekly rituals that either increase or decrease your resting level of happiness, or baseline. In addition, you can choose activities that make your happiness level to spike or take a nosedive. My goal is to inspire you to always prioritize your resting level of happiness!

Make Personal Happiness Your Priority and Life Philosophy

It's important to be very familiar with what happiness feels like in your mind, body, and soul. Be cognizant of the emotions you feel during sustained periods of happiness and how you choose to live your days. Use this connection and knowledge of self as your guiding compass. As I mentioned previously, you might be thinking, "I haven't really felt that happy since I was a young child." This is completely okay. You must become very connected to the pleasant emotions and periods of your life in order to use them as a guide. How you do this is by creating quiet space and time for inner reflection and through communication. You can journal, talk to a therapist, coach, friend, or family member. Write down or talk about the happiest moments in your life and communicate what made you feel happy and what emotions you felt. Use this compass to guide your decision-making, and never let go of your intention to live a happy life.

Accept that you cannot and will not always be in what's considered "high" emotional states. Life is full of ups and downs, and some are extremely challenging and difficult. However, as I have shown you with stories of my dad choosing happiness after divorce and my choosing to leave Calgary in search of a happier and more fulfilling life, you can go through a really rough period in your life and still live a happy life overall.

Wake up every single day and remind yourself that you are mortal. After opening your eyes, think of one thing that you are excited about for the day—something that brings a smile to your face. You don't know what will happen today or tomorrow, and any one of us can be gone in the blink of an eye. When my children were really young, I had a health scare. I remember lying in the hospital bed with a nurse hovering over me. Silent tears were streaming down my face as I thought, "Who is going to take care of my little girls?" It scared every part of my being. Since then, I never have forgotten that every day is a gift. If you were told that you had two months to live, would you be worrying about all of the problems that you are worrying about right now? Life is precious, and the world needs you to be present right now. When you are positive, caring, and optimistic, you make other people around you happy. Another misconception is that prioritizing your own happiness is somehow selfish. That's simply not true! Human energy is an open-loop circuit, and this is called "emotional contagion." Emotional contagion is the phenomenon of having one person's emotions and related behaviors directly trigger similar emotions and behaviors in other people. Your energy, whether positive or negative, spreads to others whether we like it or not. How are you showing up for the people in your life right now? Be honest with yourself. Are you being the best version of yourself for your family today?

Find Purpose and Meaning

Many people believe that they need to be living a life full of purpose in order to have a purposeful life, which isn't true. When you think about Nelson Mandela, the Dalai Lama, or Mother Teresa, you know that their lives have always been full of meaning. However, every single person on earth cannot and does not live in this manner. The majority of the people on the planet work hard to balance careers, families, and daily life. Every day of your life does not need to be filled with meaning in order to live a life of meaning and purpose.

What aspects of work and life do you truly love and that make you feel great? What do you enjoy about being alive? Here are a few examples of both personal and professional aspects of life that give people meaning:

- **Personal:** spending time with friends and family, reading, traveling, hiking, cooking, listening to music, dancing, watching great movies, taking photos, going to restaurants, meditating, playing guitar, caring for elderly parents, donating time to a local charity, and engaging in spiritual practices and spiritual connection
- **Professional:** mentoring, learning, accomplishing a big project, public speaking, working on a great team, attending conferences, networking, writing, creating new products or experiences, being mentored, brainstorming, and interacting socially with colleagues

What do you enjoy about life right now? Dr. Ben-Shahar taught me that we need to spend only an hour a week doing meaningful and purposeful activities in order to create a positive effect for the rest of the week. Of course, you can spend more time doing these activities if you so choose, but it's not absolutely necessary. The idea is to learn exactly what gives you a sense of meaning and to be aware that it does. Compared to others, individuals who lead purpose-filled lives are also more likely to report high levels of life satisfaction. From adolescence to late adulthood, individuals with purpose report feeling more satisfied with their lives.[11] Reflect on the last 6 – 12 months of your life and take notice of what is giving you meaning and purpose. If you feel that there is an opportunity to increase the meaning that you feel and experience, make a list of all the activities and aspects of life that you truly love. Think back to the reminder of being mortal. If you weren't alive anymore and were looking back on your life, what would you miss? Being connected to purpose in your life has wonderful benefits not only for your happiness, but for your health as well!

Cherish Your Physical Body

Both my parents were active skiers, and as my sisters and I were growing up, they taught us to love the sport. I remember watching my dad water-ski, skimming the lake where we spent our summers. My mother taught us to cherish our physical bodies through our daily activities. I'm forever thankful to her for demonstrating the importance of daily movement and healthy nutrition as a part of life. Although I didn't realize it at the time, her exercise habits that I witnessed as a child are a massive source of happiness for me. She danced and performed Jane Fonda cardio workouts in our living room, went for runs in the neighborhood, golfed, and swam. When I had soccer practice, it wasn't uncommon to see my mom doing squats on the sidelines. She constantly was moving, staying healthy and strong.

How connected do you feel to your physical body? Can you see a difference in your mental performance after exercising? Movement isn't something that I do, it's a part of who I am. Exercise is one of my top priorities. I know how well I feel when I incorporate movement into my day, and I know the difference when I don't. Yes, exercise is important to having a strong immune system and gives you self-confidence, but one of the key reasons I exercise is that it makes me happier!

We are creatures on this planet, just like animals. We're not meant to sit at desks all day, then in a car, then on couches. Not incorporating movement into your daily life is the equivalent of waking up and taking a depressant pill. There's a direct connection linked between your exercise level and your happiness level. The mind and body are interconnected, and the benefits of movement on your brain, body, and outlook in life are countless. Exercise increases the levels of serotonin, norepinephrine, and dopamine—all important transmitters that traffic our thoughts and emotions.

The Science of Exercise and the Brain

Everyone should read the book John Ratey, MD, authored, *Spark: The Revolutionary New Science of Exercise and the Brain*. A leading researcher on the effects of exercise and the brain, Dr. Ratey has proven through multiple studies and evidence that exercise directly benefits learning and decreases and/or removes stress, anxiety, depression, attention deficit, and addiction.[12] According to the World Health Organization in 2020, depression is the leading cause of disability worldwide and is a major contributor to the overall global burden of disease. I find it incredible that Dr. Ratey's information isn't well-known and taught in every single school worldwide. If it were, pharmaceutical companies wouldn't be nearly as successful with their antidepressant drugs. Your brain is where emotions are created and, thus, is the center for happiness (and unhappiness), and exercise is part of a wonder drug available to you! The other parts of the wonder drug are sleep and nutrition. I would even go as far as to say that exercise is *the most important thing* when it comes to happiness. Exercise, adequate sleep, and healthy nutrition are a must! In his book, Dr. Ratey shares fascinating studies about both children and adults that reaffirm why movement is vital, and he discusses several studies that indicate the direct correlation between exercise and happiness.

One of the best examples is a landmark research project from the Human Population Laboratory in Berkeley called the Alameda County Study. Researchers tracked 8,023 people for 26 years, surveying them about a number of factors related to lifestyle habits and healthiness, starting in 1965. They checked back in with participants in 1974 and in 1983. Of all the people with no signs of depression at the beginning, those who became inactive over the next 9 years were 1.5 times more likely to have depression by 1983 than their counterparts.

The Effect of Food

While I'm not a nutritionist or food expert, my mother demonstrated balance when I was growing up, and I choose to live my life in the same way. I eat fresh fruits and vegetables daily, buy whole grains, and eat healthy proteins. I'm very aware of the connection between my brain and my stomach. By this I mean, knowing it takes around 20 minutes for my brain to register fullness, I am conscious of when my stomach feels full. Of course, I'm not perfect, and I love sweets and salty snacks, too! My intention, however, is balance and moderation. I recognize how eating a lot of really unhealthy food makes me feel and how it changes my perspective on life. I feel much better when I eat healthy food. Feeling happy is extremely important to me, as I am sure you have guessed by now.

Food can make us feel happy or sad and is very important to how you feel and the kind of life you live. Take, for example, the Blue Zones located in Sardinia, Italy; the islands of Okinawa, Japan; Nicoya Peninsula in Costa Rica; Ikaria, Greece; and Loma Linda, California. In these five regions, people typically live longer than average and with fewer chronic diseases. Author, educator, and researcher Dan Buettner discovered and named these regions the Blue Zones. He found that these zones have nine similarities, and he titled them "Power 9":

1. Move Naturally
2. Purpose
3. Down Shift (as it relates to stress)

4. The 80% Rule (eat until you are 80% full)
5. Plant Slant (diet)
6. Wine at 5 (moderation)
7. Belong
8. Loved Ones First
9. The Right Tribe (your social circle)

People who live in these five Blue Zones also have similar diets that directly contribute to their health and happiness. These diets range from a plant-based diet incorporating beans to diets low in beef and dairy and high in tea. Fruits, vegetables, whole grains, and healthy proteins are key to how we feel daily and are part of the Blue Zones similarities.

Happiness Sleep

Sleep is also crucial to happiness! You have read it, heard it, and you probably know that sleep is good for you. Everyone has heard of beauty sleep; well, I call it "happiness sleep." When I don't get seven to eight hours of great sleep, I'm not a nice person. It's really that simple. My personality changes and not for the better. Just like with exercise, it's extremely difficult to have a joyful and calm day when you're tired or, worse yet, exhausted. Yes, you're likely preoccupied with numerous priorities from work and your personal life and want to turn your brain off by watching television or scrolling social media—I get it. The challenge is that when you choose to do that and not get the appropriate amount of sleep, you're not as effective at work or as a leader. It affects your decision-making, creativity, memory, and critical thinking. Not enough sleep affects your personal life as it makes you more irritable, short-tempered, and less patient and resilient, and it negatively affects your relationships because you communicate differently.

According to an article titled, "Sleep Disorders and Sleep Deprivation: An Unmet Public Health Problem" from the Institute of Medicine (U.S.) Committee on Sleep Medicine and Research, the authors found that "sleep problems, difficulty initiating and maintaining sleep, nonrestorative sleep, and excessive daytime sleepiness are associated with adverse effects on well-being, functioning, and quality of life, according to numerous studies covering the general population."[13] You need consistent and healthy sleep habits for your career, your health, and your happiness.

Regularly exercising, eating balanced and nutritious foods, and consistently getting enough sleep directly connect to your happiness and your psychological well-being. I tell clients and groups that it's actually very difficult to feel really happy if you do not make these the three top priorities in life. While many people exercise and attempt to eat healthily because they want to look physically attractive, I feel that that goal is too narrow and often doesn't create enough motivation internally. When you think of the term "wellness," physiques of models likely come to mind, due to the abounding marketing messages. Going forward, when you think of good food, sleep, and exercise, envision a joyful and energetic happy person. When you're happy, you're more likely to achieve your health and wellness goals and are also likely to inspire your friends, family, and coworkers to do the same.

Cultivate Human Connection

As stated previously, the number one predictor of happiness for people around the globe is human connection. It's true across all cultures, religions, and ethnicities. People thrive when connected to others. Being connected means spending time with those whom they care about and who care about them. A World Happiness Report annually surveys and measures life satisfaction in over 140 countries. Year after year, Scandinavian countries like Denmark, Norway, and Finland are declared the happiest countries. Citizens in these countries spend a tremendous amount of time forming and supporting their connections with friends and family. They leave work by five o'clock daily in order to play sports, have dinner, or spend time with those they care about.

One of the most fascinating studies on life and happiness is the 80-plus-year-old Harvard Grant Study. Years ago, I watched the TED Talk about this study, and I was instantly in awe and connected to the story and research findings.

Beginning in 1938, scientists tracked the health and lifestyles of 268 Harvard sophomores. There were various control groups, one being a group of 456 Boston inner-city residents; they called the inner-city resident group the "Glueck Study". The overarching Harvard Grant Study researched, tracked, and monitored all areas of the groups' lives, work, relationships, and health. "The surprising finding is that our relationships and how happy we are in our relationships has a powerful influence on our health," said Robert Waldinger, director of the study and a psychiatrist at Massachusetts General Hospital and a professor of psychiatry at Harvard Medical School. "Taking care of your body is important but tending to your relationships is a form of self-care, too. That, I think, is the revelation." Close relationships, more than money or fame, are what keep people happy throughout their lives, the study revealed.

Friends and family have always been a priority for me. Throughout my career, I made sure to schedule in time to connect with them on both weeknights and the weekends. Whether it was going out to eat, dance, watch a movie, or explore, making time to connect with others has always been a part of my life. Having fun is really important. Try new experiences and choose to be around people who are fun and want to enjoy life as well.

If I find there's someone in my life who is negative and consistently drains my energy, I create boundaries within that relationship. I choose not to let that person suck away my energy. Sometimes, this can be a lot more difficult if it's a family member, but you still can choose to give that person a lot of your emotional self while protecting your inner energy. How you do this is to write down a list of the people who are draining your energy or giving you negative energy. Then brainstorm on ways that you could limit your time and communication with them. These are boundaries. The next step is to choose which of these boundaries you can and want to commit to.

As you go through life, there will be times when you need to "shake your tree." You must stand tall, grounded in your truth, and "shake off," or let go of, those negative people in your life. It may sound really harsh, but I believe letting them go is necessary for you to live a healthy and happy life. Your choices directly impact your happiness, and you must be selective in choosing your social circle. Create one that lifts you up and inspires you to be a better person.

Live with Awe

Do not take your daily life for granted. You aren't immortal. Waking up daily is not a guarantee. Every day that you and your family and friends wake up should be treated as a gift.

Choose to be filled with awe in this life. Awe is an emotion of wonder inspired by authority or by the sacred or sublime. This emotion is the perception of vastness or feeling small. Do you feel connected to Mother Nature? Do you recognize the miracles that happen on the planet daily all around you? I might have more awe embedded in my personality because I grew up in the woods in Northern Canada, surrounded by nature's wonders. I learned early to be thankful for what I experience each day and to pause, look up at the sky, hear the birds chirping in the morning, and take in the beauty of the flowers blooming in my neighborhood.

Travel is also a huge source of awe in my life, and studies have proven that such experiences bring you more happiness than material possessions. Those moments of awe are enormous when you experience some of Earth's incredible creations. I choose to hold these visions in my mind and also to find awe in watching videos, hearing stories, being outside, and reading books.

In the 2019 research article titled, "The Proximal Experience of Awe," researchers explain that the emotion of awe is classified as a self-transcendent emotion and is associated with self-diminishment.[14] In the study, participants watched Earth from outer space on a television and via virtual reality. In addition to feeling awe, the participants reported increases in feelings of gratitude, compassion, optimism, and love. They felt self-relevant thoughts, where they saw themselves in relation to the world and others, and they reported feelings of greater connectedness and humility. The authors said, "People experience awe in the midst of anything perceived as larger than the self (i.e., vast) that challenges current mental structures."

Feeling awe directs our attention outward and reminds us that we are a small part of this world and universe. Unhappiness comes from focusing too much on ourselves and thinking we are the center. I encourage you to find and feel awe in your life. You may not be able to go up in space and look down at Earth, but there are tremendous gifts that can give you this emotion in your daily life.

Continuous Improvement

Children spend the majority of their day learning and growing—they are sponges soaking up knowledge. Their brains expand as they take in as much new information as they can. Once children become adults, the majority of them do not prioritize learning as much as they should. Yes, when many people start new positions, they must go through the onboarding process and learn about their organization and job requirements. Many make progress in their career paths and continue to rise in the industry, but they don't dedicate time to continuously educate themselves. Learning can be about anything! It can be professional or personal. I know that I instantly felt happier when I began studying coaching and positive psychology, even though it added time and work to my already full plate. Take the time to continue your education.

You can take in-person or online classes and learn from mentors, therapists, or coaches. Stretch yourself by reading books and watching TED Talks. Learning also can occur by spending dedicated time with your boss and colleagues and focusing on personal development. You can choose to learn to play a new instrument, speak a new language, to cook, or to garden. Find areas of life that are interesting and exciting to you, then dedicate time in your week to learn and grow. I promise, learning will make you happier! It has always given me a lot of energy and increased my excitement for life.

The SPIRE Model of Well-Being

I learned about the SPIRE Model of Well-Being from the Happiness Studies Academy's Dr. Ben-Shahar. He taught two of the largest classes in Harvard University's history: *Positive Psychology* and *The Psychology of Leadership*. Today, he consults and lectures around the world to executives from multinational corporations, the general public, and at-risk populations. The topics he lectures on include leadership, happiness, education, innovation, ethics, self-esteem, resilience, goal setting, and mindfulness. His books have been translated into more than 25 languages and have appeared on best-seller lists around the world. Dr. Ben-Shahar is the cofounder and chief learning officer of *Happiness Studies Academy, Potentialife*, a nine-month leadership development program, Maytiv Center for Positive Psychology, and *Happier.TV*.

I spent an entire year studying his model in detail. Under each area, there is a wide variety of topics. It is not possible to reteach the whole method here, but I'll provide you with some of the key take-aways. It's a holistic approach to human happiness, and I've taught this model and all the topics under each area to people for years.

I interviewed Dr. Ben-Shahar on my "Arrive At Happy Leaders" show, where he stated:

"SPIRE has to do with the definition of happiness. It is based on research and thinking from Eastern and Western thinkers from the past and the present. Happiness comprises of five elements. They are spiritual well-being, which is finding a sense of meaning and about being present in the here and now. It is about physical well-being, the mind-body connection. It is about exercise, sleep recovery, and nutrition. Then it is about intellectual well-being, which is about cultivating a curious mindset and deep learning. There is a connection between mental and physical health and curiosity. People who ask questions and who are lifelong learners actually live longer. Then there is the relational aspect of well-being. Relationships are, of course, important for happiness. Finally, emotional well-being, dealing with painful emotions and cultivating pleasurable emotions. It is important to think about SPIRE on the individual level and the organizational level.

"When people think of happiness, they often think that it is for the good times. They believe that when things are not going well, we should park happiness. Happiness is important when things are going well, but when life is challenging and negative, the science of happiness can play a very important role. Why? Because it can help us become more resilient. It can help us deal with situations better, and in many ways the science of happiness is about creating resilience and a strong psychological immune system. Having a strong immune system doesn't mean we don't get sick. It simply means we get sick less often. And when we do, we recover more promptly. This is how happiness can help us now, especially when we are going through difficult times."

Spiritual well-being is connected to our personal happiness, because it allows us to live with the daily awareness that we are a small part of a universal whole. The Dalai Lama has said, "The majority of human suffering comes from thinking too much about ourselves." When we are connected spiritually and feel that our lives have meaning and purpose, we have a greater sense of inner peace, calm, and joy. Spiritual well-being can be the religion in your life, but it doesn't have to be. The mind and body are 100 percent connected at all times.

Taking care of your physical body with nutritious balanced food, healthy sleep, exercise, hydration, and hugs is proven to make you a happier human. Another aspect of your physical well-being is the health of your mind, your psychological health. For example, if you have healthy ways to recover from stress throughout the day and on the weekends, pain and negative aspects from built-up stress won't exist in your physical body. When you go through a challenging time in your life and you talk to someone and/or journal about it, your physical body becomes healthier and, in turn, you become happier.

As humans, we're designed and programmed to learn. We thrive emotionally and psychologically when we grow and stretch ourselves. Intellectual well-being occurs when our mind, body, and soul expand. Like the children in your life, you can also be a sponge! Just because you're an adult doesn't mean that you can no longer learn. We become happier when we partake in what Dr. Ben-Shahar calls "ReflAction." It's an ongoing process of action and reflection, action, then more reflection. Happiness increases when you are curious and open and ask questions. We cannot be reflective all the time; we need to reflect and then act over and over.

As I've stated, relationships, or human connections, are the number one predictor of happiness. All relationships stem from the one that you have with yourself. The happiest people in the world spend more time with their friends and family every day and every week. Happiness increases when you are open and allow yourself to be known and when you really get to know the people in your life. Connecting is an ongoing process.

Happiness (or unhappiness) can also stem from romantic relationships in our lives. The Gottman Institute is one of the leading research institutes on relationships. It teaches couples how to have thriving relationships that bring lasting joy. Relational well-being comes from tending to both your professional and personal relationships and putting in continuous effort throughout your life.

Emotional well-being is an area that when I was studying it, I thought, "Wow! This would have been really useful information to learn as a teenager." Everyone has pleasant and painful emotions; it's a part of being human. Accepting our emotions is key to happiness, along with observing them in a nonjudgmental way. When we have painful emotions, such as fear or anxiety, and don't give ourselves permission to feel how we feel, we can feel bad. Learn how to view your painful emotions as teachers. Instead of feeling bad that you have these "negative emotions" like anger, guilt, and anxiety, change your perspective and ask yourself, "What is this emotion trying to teach me?" Dr. Ben-Shahar's notion of giving yourself the "permission to be human" will change your life. I teach it to everyone who attends my trainings, keynote talks, and executive retreats. The human experience is an emotional roller coaster of successes and obstacles, so give yourself permission to know and understand it. Studies have shown that when we communicate our emotions and "let them out" through talking and journaling, it makes us happier.

The New Neuroscience of Emotions

After becoming interested in adult neuroplasticity from my positive psychology studies, I earned my Certificate in Neuroscience from Dr. Irena O'Brien, PhD, and The Neuroscience School. I share many neuroscience topics throughout this book. One of the most fascinating areas for happiness and successful leadership centers around emotions. Dr. Lisa Feldman Barrett has studied emotions and neuroscience for over 25 years and is at the forefront of the new neuroscience of emotion. In her TED Talk, Dr. Barrett says, "Emotions are guesses that your brain constructs in the moment where billion of brain cells are working together." Our brains use past experiences and the physical sensations in our body to create emotions based on predictions. She shares that "our brains predict and construct our experience of the world." It feels as if emotions *happen* to us, when in reality, they are *created* by us. Meaning, when you are stressed, angry, or overwhelmed, for example, you should tune in to your body and ask yourself, "Could this emotion have a purely physical cause?" You could be tired and/or hungry. You have the ability to construct experiences differently.

Under each of the above SPIRE (spiritual, physical, intellectual, relational, and emotional) areas of your life, proven evidence-based strategies and behaviors exist that can increase your happiness. Think of these areas as levers to pull, where the idea is not to be perfect or achieve greatness in all areas at the same time.

You might want to focus on your relationships or prioritize learning something new this year, for example. A wealth of information and inspiration can be gained from this model, and I encourage you to learn more.

When was the last time that you reflected on your own happiness? How often do you pause and reflect on how happy you are? As you go through life, it's imperative that you stop and look back at your life. You need to know where you are in order to determine where you want to go.

Focusing on your personal happiness is so important! You're on this journey with me for a reason, and we are just getting started. I know you want to be successful, healthy, and mentally well. Get ready to learn seven more steps to help you achieve just that!

Happy Leader Prompts

1. Schedule sleep, movement, and healthy nutrition in your daily calendar. Place four physical reminders around your home and work environments to remind you to prioritize sleep, movement, and healthy nutrition daily.

2. Write down specifically how much time you are spending connecting with friends and family on a weekly basis. What is the ideal amount of time that you would like to spend with them weekly?

3. What do you want to learn in the next 12 months? Make a. list and choose what you want to commit to.

CHAPTER 7:

Step Two—Zoom Out

To zoom out comes from the field of photography. It is the adjustment of the lens of a camera so that the image seems to be smaller and farther away. Photographers zoom out to get the widest possible view of the scene. To leaders, it means to have a broad perspective and to view the entire organization and system, not just the area that is their responsibility. A broad perspective allows leaders to see divisions, challenges, and opportunities from many different angles, which positively affects decision making. Every division or department is interconnected in business and in all organizations. When you master the ability to zoom out, you view the organization like your boss or the company's owner(s), enabling yourself to become aligned with them. When you research information and communicate via email or in person, you can then tackle interdepartmental challenges from the right perspective. Your boss will also know that you are located at the right vantage point. Your peers in the organization also will respect and appreciate you.

Zooming Out Matters

I learned from my experiences in Hawaii, New York City, Istanbul, and Los Angeles that the best business skills are listening and asking questions. You should never assume that you understand what's happening in other areas of the organization. Whenever another leader came to speak to me about challenges that my department was causing their department, I took out my notebook and pen and listened intently. When you remove your defensiveness and the need to be right, you build strong bonds with your coworkers, which makes work life a lot more enjoyable. Gather all the information from your peers and then devise a plan with your team or bring all the teams together to create an action plan together. Your peers will respect you more, and the business will move forward faster. To set the example of alignment and respect, do your very best to not talk negatively about colleagues in the organization in front of your team.

When you zoom out and figuratively review the organization with a wide lens, you absolutely make better decisions. You understand the ripple effect of your team's strategies and tactics. Spend time at the beginning of a new position to gain understanding of your peers' high-level goals and the strengths and weaknesses of their team. It saves you time and effort and enables you to coach your team members on how to do the exact same. Zooming out also enables you to become a stronger communicator in executive meetings because you are able to see the business from your peers' perspective, and this builds trust and teamwork at the executive level.

Zooming out makes your job more interesting and engaging! Although you might not be the top executive or own the company, it doesn't mean that you don't need to operate like one. Take the time to understand your organization; you'll find it fascinating. There might be parts of your job that seem boring to you, but when you keep this perspective in mind, you will always be connected to the bigger picture.

Have an Owner's Perspective

I always cared about my team the most, and I believe it's natural for a leader to do so. In caring, you build closer relationships with your team members and feel responsible for their successes. What I learned over my 14 years of being a team leader is that you are more successful when you care for *all* an organization's divisions, not just your own. When another division is challenged, these challenges are yours as well. All areas of the business affect you and your team. If you have the ability to support your peers in any way, do so, as the payoff is well worth all your effort.

How do you develop an owner's perspective? Here are some strategies and tactics you can use: Obtain a very clear understanding of the owner's goals by asking clarifying questions and keeping those goals in mind. Attend ongoing meetings with your boss so that you always know her top priorities. Consistently communicate with your peers. Keep the top goals and priorities of the company's owner(s), your boss, and your peers in mind as you create strategic plans with your team. If you're ever unsure if you have the right perspective, check in with your boss and be direct about your intentions.

Connecting to clear, motivating goals is a crucial aspect of positive and successful leadership. Obtain a deep understanding of the short- and long-term goals for each area of the company.

Then, communicate this big picture to your team on a regular basis. Each team member can make better decisions if they know where the organization is going as a whole. They will look more informed and stronger when they are communicating to others in the company. Your boss and peers will clearly see that you are communicating well with your team. Communication of the goals to your team will enable them to develop a broad perspective and contribute to their professional development.

Here's an example about how zooming out and having an owner perspective can lead to massive success. I once interviewed Wendy Luttrell for my Arrive At Happy podcast. She was hired to be the CEO for Bedhead Pajamas, a high-end $4 million specialty pajama company based in Los Angeles that sold to specialty stores and one high-end Beverly Hills hotel. The owner, Renee Bertrand, hired Wendy and had very specific goals in mind.

Bertrand was a very creative designer and started Bedhead Pajamas when she was 45 years old. She really enjoyed the design part of the company but didn't enjoy any other aspects of running a business. Thus, she hired Luttrell to grow the company and to create an exit strategy for herself.

Luttrell interviewed Bertrand on her very first day on the job. She asked, "What exactly do you want to have happen? Where do you see yourself in five years?"

Bertrand explained that she wanted to retire in five years on a piece of land with her husband in Northern California. Luttrell dove deeper, asking about what that would look like monetarily and confirmed that Bertrand wanted to sell the company. Luttrell then knew exactly where the owner was currently, where she wanted to go in the future, and understood the owner's perspective. She was able to see the business and objectives through

Bertrand's eyes, and Bertrand knew that Luttrell understood and was aligned.

Over the next five years, Luttrell grew Bedhead Pajamas and always kept Bertrand's intention and goals in mind. She successfully grew a partnership with Neiman Marcus, creating products just for them, in addition to marketing and selling a Christmas overnight experience in the store for a group of six! They ended up selling six of these packages for $10,000 each, then created many successful lines of girl's pajamas for them. Over five years, Luttrell built a $4 million business with Neiman Marcus and solidified Bedhead Pajamas as a brand. She grew the company's worth to $13 million, enabling Bertrand to successfully sell the company and retire in the time frame that she had requested.

Chief executive officers and other leaders can have their own agenda in organizations, which absolutely can create challenges. Luttrell could've chosen to work towards a variety of different goals that could have served her best as CEO. She could've focused on brand building or obtaining an aggressive market share or near-term profits, to name a few. Instead, she held an in-depth conversation with the owner as a first step, learned the owner's goals, then developed and executed a plan that delivered those goals. Always keeping the owner's perspective and needs your top priority will support you in being successful.

Do you currently have a passion for a business as if it were your own? How would your job and life change if you had tighter relationships with your peers and the stakeholders? Learn to be consciously curious!

Conscious Curiosity

I've always approached business and my career in the same way that I approach studying—filled with curiosity. My perspective is that I don't know anything until I have experienced it, and even then, there are different experiences. Openness and a desire to always be learning can take you very far in your career. My interest in learning as much as I could was not driven by how much money I could make or a certain desired title, but by my keen interest to collect knowledge. Wherever I go, I carry a notebook and pen and write copious notes. Think of all the people in your industry and in your organization as teachers who have something to share with you.

Always ask questions. I believe that you cannot ask too many questions in your career and in life. When you receive an answer from your boss, a stakeholder, or executives, and you don't fully understand and need more information, dive deeper until you do. Have a sense of what to ask at each level of the organization, and always use your time with regional and divisional leaders to learn as much as possible. Have the intention to grow yourself and to view an organization from different angles. When you don't agree with another's perspective, ask questions to really understand what contributes to their view. Understand that each person's background, experiences, and goals affect their view, and be curious about how and why they see things as they do.

Spend time understanding the priorities and goals of each of the leaders with whom you work. You need to be able to see the organization from their perspective. Such conversations should happen when you first start your role and should continue as long as you are a member of an organization. Write down each leader's goals and priorities, then review your notes. When a team member faces obstacles and challenges with another company division, share with them that division's goals and find a place of understanding versus creating a culture of us versus them.

One of the biggest lessons that I learned throughout my career was to not take complaints personally from anyone else in an organization. This is very difficult to do when you are just beginning your career and don't have a lot of confidence or experience. It doesn't mean you cannot do it; it just means it will take more intention and effort on your part. Some people are simply better at communicating than others. Others are much stronger at being aware of their emotions, managing them, and being proactive instead of reactive. Many times, I've been the target of stress and anger from other people. I have learned to observe events instead of diving right into them headfirst. Learn to reflect on situations that involve other people and know that it isn't always about you. Consciously choosing to pause, reflect, then act is one strength that will carry you far in your career and in life. Practicing mindfulness will support you in gaining this skill. (Mindfulness is the act of maintaining a nonjudgmental state of heightened awareness of your thoughts, emotions, or experiences from moment to moment.) Just remember, nothing in your career revolves around you. An organization is a group of people moving in the same direction, so learn how to not take anything personally.

Raise the Bar

Once you have an understanding of each division within your organization and of the company as a whole, you can begin creating strategies on how to make it better. One way to do this is to be highly engaged in every leadership meeting and forum. Take these meetings seriously, and approach them with the mindset of "How can I contribute and make us more successful?" It's your responsibility to ensure that the meetings and calls you attend add value to you and that you add value to them. Approach these meetings with that ownership perspective and speak up when you hear another leader contradict the organization's long-term goals. It's your choice to make leadership meetings and calls interactive, interesting, and useful, not just something on your calendar that you need to attend.

I always bring new ideas for the entire organization to meetings. I challenge everyone to evolve and achieve more personally and in their respective areas. Be your peers' cheerleader and push them to achieve more! When you are fully engaged in the company, even if you're not in your dream role, work is a lot more interesting.

Be customer centric. Yes, I was a director of sales and marketing for 14 years, so customers were my life. When every leader in the organization cares about their customers wholeheartedly and with dedicated passion, a business will soar. Throughout my career, I worked with leaders of different divisions that understood this and others who didn't. For example, I encountered financial leaders who were aligned and supported the hotels to better attract and retain the customers, and others who did not. Remind yourself, your peers, and your team that your customers are your company. When it comes to your customers, how are you raising the bar right now?

I was the director of marketing and public relations for the W Istanbul Hotel in Turkey for two years. This work and life experience was one of the best in my life—a huge adventure filled with incredible people, cultures, and memories—and it challenged and stretched me in many ways. In my role, I was responsible for creating brand awareness and generating demand for the rooms, suites, meetings, events, restaurants, and the nightclub. I knew the W brand very well, because my previous position was leading the sales team for the five W Hotels in New York City. By this point, I had been working in hotels for a decade and was familiar with operations as well. My husband and I had moved to Istanbul together, and he was the general manager of the hotel. Our company had allowed us to transfer to Istanbul together, and we managed to work independently from each other while supporting each other at the same time. We were the only non-Turkish people working at the W Istanbul, and the majority of the customers were from the United States and Western Europe and spoke English.

In this role, I went above and beyond to zoom out and view the business from the perspective of the Turkish owner and the hotel management company. I wanted to add as much value as I possibly could. For example, I volunteered to be the weekend manager on duty as much as possible. This work didn't fall under marketing or public relations, but it benefited the hotel greatly.

I spent hours on the weekends in the small, chic, dark lobby of the hotel connecting with the hourly employees and guests. The front door looked out on Akaretler, the traditional Ottoman row houses where the employees of the old Dolmabahçe Palace lived. The streets were cobblestone, and the W was tucked away in that area. Our lobby smelled of yummy candles and was hot in the summer and cold in the winter, like the weather of the city.

I can remember one specific exchange with an international guest in the lobby. I was the manager on duty, and I had greeted the guest warmly as he walked through the front door.

"Hi. Welcome to the W Istanbul. How was your trip into the city?"

"Wow! The drivers here are insane. I don't think I have ever been in that fast a cab!"

I laughed and replied, "I know. The traffic and drivers in Istanbul take some getting used to. Where are you traveling from?"

"New York. This is my second time to the city. Here for work."

"I love New York and used to live there. I know you are about to check in, and I don't want to keep you waiting, but please let me know if there is anything, I can do to make your stay and visit to Istanbul more comfortable. My name is Tia, and I'm the director of marketing."

"Amazing. Thank you so much. My name is Keith. You don't sound Turkish."

"No, I am Canadian/American and have lived here for six months. It's an incredible city and country, and I hope you have time to discover some of my secret places in the city."

"That would be great! Thank you so much, Tia."

I had such small exchanges with customers every single week. I learned about their negative experiences in the hotel and in the city and tried to turn them around as fast as I could. I brought all the negative customer experiences to the management and executive teams so we could do everything possible to ensure that such problems did not happen to others. I observed how the front office, spa, restaurants, nightclub, housekeeping, employee cafeteria, and human resources operated. I listened closely to the employees and customers and acted where improvements could be made. I knew that business inside and out and became a voice of leadership, a voice for the customer, and a voice for the employees. At times, it caused challenges between me and other leaders in the hotel who didn't appreciate the fact that I was "looking under their hood" so to speak. Yet, I understood their perspective and prioritized our relationship and tried to communicate in a way so that they didn't take any feedback personally. I focused on the challenges and behaviors instead of the person.

Choosing to view an organization from a wider perspective and different perspectives increases your personal happiness and professional success in several ways. It strengthens the relationships you have with others in the organization and increases your human connection. You will progress more towards your individual goals and the company's goals. Progress in meaningful work gives us motivation and increases our pleasant emotions.[15] In *The Book of Joy* by the Dalai Lama and Desmond Tutu, the Dalai Lama says, "For every event in life, there are many different angles. When you look at the same event from a wider perspective, your sense of worry and anxiety reduces, and you have greater joy." Here, he uses the term "wider perspective," which involves stepping back, within our own mind, to look at the bigger picture and to move beyond our limited self-awareness and our limited self-interest. Choosing to be curious about all areas of an organization taps into your intellectual well-being. When you have the perspective of a lifelong learner by having conscious curiosity, you find more joy in your work. Positive psychology's approach, called "appreciative inquiry," is a collaborative strengths-based approach to change in organizations. This approach focuses on what is working, what you can learn from what is working, and how you can apply it to other areas of an organization. The example of appreciative inquiry shows how to be curious in a way that is supportive and collaborative. When you raise the bar, do your personal best, and motivate others to do the same, you feel pride and excitement. When you exhibit authentic pride—belief in yourself and in your work— you are more likely to demonstrate extroversion, agreeableness, genuine self-esteem, self-confidence, and conscientiousness—all adaptive, appealing traits for work!

This is Step Two of eight, and I know that you can master the perspective of zooming out. You can have more joy, calm, fun, and excitement once you learn how to operate in this way. Your feelings of stress, anxiety about the future, and fear will reduce because you know that you're leading with the correct vantage point of the business. You will no longer feel out of control but instead feel connected to others and the company as a whole. In any leadership role, the stakes are high, and you must take it seriously. In doing so, you will receive positive feedback, and it will be reflected in your reviews and compensation. You can absolutely zoom out and lead like an owner!

Happy Leader Prompts

1. What are your owner's goals, beliefs, and needs? If you do not know them exactly, find out and write them down.
2. What are the priorities and goals of each of your peers? If you do not know them exactly, find out and write them down.
3. How can you raise the bar and expectations for yourself, your team, and your organization?

CHAPTER 8:

Step Three—Execute Brilliantly

t was 8:45 P.M., and I was still in my tiny cubicle at the W Court Hotel on 39th Street and Lexington Avenue in New York City. I had been there since 7:30 A.M., and there was no end in sight. My email in-box was overflowing, and I felt as if there were endless projects that needed my immediate attention. I stood up, stretched my arms above my head, and looked around. "What an environment," I thought.

Black and gray exposed wires crisscrossed along the ceiling. My dark gray L-shaped cubicle and the fluorescent lights from above created a jail-cell-type setting. The office smelled of a mix of carpet odors, food, and stale who knows what. It was completely silent, except for the hum of my computer. I snacked on popcorn and sparkling water from a local bodega and knew that it wasn't healthy.

"When am I going to be finished?" I said out loud to no one. I was the associate director of sales for five W Hotels in Manhattan.

I led the group sales team and had a sales market of my own. Oh, and did I mention that I moved to New York in 2008, when the market crashed, and New York was the epicenter? Our five hotels were struggling, and that was an understatement!

At this point in my career, I hadn't yet mastered the principles of "execute brilliantly." I believed that hours worked equaled success. I was a perfectionist who also believed that working on everything is how you moved the needle forward. However, the goal and desired intention of this chapter is to teach and inspire you to execute brilliantly without having to work 15-hour days and weekends. It's your choice if you want to do that, but it's just that—your choice. Many leaders around the globe operate with a working-nonstop operating system. I now know that with organization, prioritization, self-confidence, and speed, every leader can have a hugely successful career and a fun, balanced personal life as well.

What are the five big goals for the position that you are in right now? Can you answer that question quickly off the top of your head? What does success look like for you in this position? Are you crystal clear on what this success looks like?

Do you ever have "analysis paralysis" and are challenged moving work and projects forward? "Analysis paralysis" is the idea that overanalyzing or overthinking a situation can cause forward motion or decision-making to become paralyzed, meaning that no solution or course of action is decided upon. Do you feel that you are bogged down by projects and other people's to-do lists?

To *execute brilliantly* means that you are efficient and accurate in executing your job. When you execute brilliantly, you don't need to work nonstop, and you have balance in your life. The following are my proven strategies so you can learn how to execute brilliantly and successfully. Master these strategies and change how you work forever.

The Benefits of Speed

Why does speed matter when it comes to leadership? As a leader, you must accomplish many different objectives. You are balancing the needs of stakeholders, your boss, your peers, and the needs of the team(s) you lead. Competition is always present, and it's up to you to stay one step ahead. If you don't move quickly, your team will not move quickly. Speed allows you to accomplish your work, analyze the success, pivot, and keep going. You truly cannot afford to move slowly in today's business world. It's imperative that you execute your job quickly and that you execute it well. It's completely fine to make mistakes. Of course, you don't want to be making mistakes all the time, or certainly not making the same mistakes repeatedly. Recognize, however, that mistakes mean you are trying. When your intentions are clear, and you are in a team culture, you will analyze, learn, and grow from your efforts.

Create Plans and Take Action

Numerous planning templates are available. I have used the SMART plan template for years and find it useful. The SMART Plan is a one-page document with five columns (Specific, Measurable, Achievable, Realistic, and Time-Bound). The plan is used to create clear strategies with accountability and due dates for larger goals that you are looking to accomplish. I have used this template whenever I've had a short-medium goal that needed to be met or beat, and all of my direct reports have utilized this tool as well. Keep your templates to a maximum of one page each and create them with your boss, peers, and direct reports. List your big goal at the top of the page along with any big metrics that align with the goal. Then, brainstorm with one or more team members about what key strategies will get you there and add this to the plan. Each specific strategy must have measurable metrics listing who is accountable, realistic steps that must be taken and by whom, and the timelines for each step. When my teams were ready to finish each step, I was famous for leading quick brainstorm huddles with different groups, and we would let the ideas fly. I suggest you also do the same. Select which strategies and tactics are the strongest from this huddle session, write up your one-page plan, and start its execution. Send your SMART Plan out to everyone involved the day it is created and place the next huddle meeting on the calendar.

Don't let stress or feelings of being overwhelmed prevent you from honing in on what you need to accomplish. Grab those you need to achieve your goal and make it a connecting and fun experience!

Stay Organized

You need to be a master at using your calendar and view it as your ally. I use different colors in its design and literally schedule everything! My brain moves pretty quickly, so I tend to forget a lot of tasks and information if I don't remind myself. Your calendar can also support your relationship, health and wellness, and personal development goals. Schedule your exercise, meditation, dinner with friends, date nights with your significant other, and even one-on-one time with your children if you have them. If you have intentions to lead, work, and live in a certain way, scheduling is one of the best ways to ensure it happens.

Write down *everything*. Throughout my career, people have teased me, saying that I look like a student, but I never cared. I am a massive notetaker who gets stuff done. When you write things down, pen to paper, you are more likely to remember the information.[16] By no means do I have a photographic memory, so this trait has served me very well, and I return to my notebooks time and again, seeking information from throughout my career.

Talk to people. Get up from your desk (and your in-box) and walk over to talk to them in person or call them on the phone. Do you really want more emails? Here is a really valuable tip that will enable you to stay organized and not drown in work:

SEND LESS EMAILS IF YOU WANT
TO RECEIVE LESS EMAILS.

It's really that simple. Yes, you need written communication, of course, but you will be amazed when you talk to colleagues and see how fast you can move work forward accurately without clogging up your in-box. Bonus: You will also build relationships with those colleagues as well!

Run efficient, productive, and motivating meetings that move your team(s) and the business forward. Each meeting needs to be organized with an agenda and key desired outcomes. Please don't waste anyone's time by not being prepared. I want you to be able to recognize, either on your own or with the help of your team(s), when you are facing a large obstacle and be able to successfully overcome it. Obstacles are not demotivators; they challenge us to get creative and find solutions.

My certification in neuroscience from The Neuroscience School taught me that we can set up our work and home environments for both maximum productivity and good choices. Know that these environments always win against human willpower. For example, if there is a leadership book that you want to read at night before you go to sleep, you will increase the likelihood of reading it if you place said book on your coffee table and see it before deciding to turn on the television.

To make your day more productive, according to neuroscience, use these strategies:

- Plan out your day.
- Exercise.
- Drink the appropriate amount of water.
- Identify your peak productive times.
- Prioritize your most important tasks when you have the most energy.
- Declutter your desk.
- Set 90 minutes aside daily for the most important tasks.
- Set deadlines for yourself. (It takes 30 minutes to focus your mind on a task.)
- Tune out noise, using calming music if there are distractions.
- Take breaks and naps.
- Be mindful of your phone use.

In addition, delegate work that needs to be completed but doesn't need to be completed by you. It can be difficult for leaders to delegate work that they are attached to and work that they feel they are the best person to complete it. I taught my teams the exercise of how to sort work into the following three columns: Accelerate, Delegate, or Eliminate. What do you need to do faster and what do you need to spend more time on? What do you need to hand over to others on your team or in the organization? What do you need to let go of or eliminate? Answering these questions and taking action enables you to remain focused and to stay organized with what you can do. Remember, the goal is to be successful and happy. You can do both!

Learn from Those Who Have Done It

Do you want to fast-track how you learn and execute? What if you had a strategy that would enable you to achieve success without struggling to figure out how? Sound too good to be true? Well, it's not. It's all about working smart versus working hard. Master that and you can avoid being overwhelmed and frustrated. In order to be successful at it, you must place your ego aside and be completely comfortable with saying, "I need help and direction." You must be comfortable learning from others and seeking out advice. Remember that for whatever you are trying to accomplish, there are people out there who have already accomplished it and did it well. It's your job to find them and learn from them.

Here is an example of how I learned from others. At one of my positions in Los Angeles, there was a business area that needed to grow and had opportunity to do so. The organization had not been successful at growing it in the past, and it was a very important part of the overall strategy for the hotel. I had some experience in this area but certainly was not an expert. I could have spent three to six months trying different tactics to see if they worked, but I didn't. Instead, I found an industry expert in this specific business area. I reached out, set up a consultation, and had her send me a detailed plan and proposal quote. I then employed the negotiation skills that I had perfected in Turkey and got her to bring down the quote. Next, I reviewed, with conviction, her credentials, plan, and price with my boss. I confidently explained that by hiring this consultant for three months, we would make a certain amount of revenue and achieve success. How could he say no? We hired her, got to work, and it was fantastic! She was a true partner and gave us specific and actionable tactics to employ, and we saw the results immediately.

Learn from people who have already been successful in what you are trying to do. There are many instances where you will not have to pay someone to support you, but if you build relationships with successful people who are ahead of you, they will be more apt to want to help later on. You can then do the same for others as you develop and grow in your career.

Create Boundaries

When I became a parent, my priorities grew and shifted. My nanny left at 5:30 P.M. daily, so I had to leave work at 5:00 P.M. and not a minute after. I learned how to focus and become razor sharp with my priorities. When you have limited time to work, you must get the right things finished; there's no other choice. I learned how to create boundaries when I became a parent, but I honestly wish I had learned this earlier on in my career. This message is not just for parents—it's for everyone. Setting boundaries can be helpful to your health, balance, relationships, and taking care of your whole self. And they are important for every single leader. I learned how to create time for healthy sleep and self-care while being an executive leader, wife, and parent. Prior to having children, I made time for fun, exercise, travel, family, romance, and downtime. You can be extremely effective and successful at work and have balance in your life. I know this because I have lived it and continue to live it today.

In order to execute accurately, creatively, and swiftly as a leader, you must make time for activities away from work. Some of your very best ideas will come when you are hiking, bike riding, or hanging with your friends. Many of my creative business solutions came to me when I wasn't at work. Reflection is a leader's best friend. It's difficult to see the business from a new perspective if you are always working in the business. Take time to reflect on your successes and challenges, and choose actions based on that contemplation. I tell every client and leadership group that I work with to use every single one of your vacation days. Incredible new insights and ideas would come to me when I was traveling the globe! Use this precious time wisely.

As a leader, you must know exactly when to say no to projects and tasks that don't align with your goals. Of course, you want to be supportive and a team player, but you are in charge of your success. When I started off as a leader, I was a "yes" person through and through. I would say yes and volunteer for every single thing that came across my desk. I didn't have that mindset, though, when I became a parent. I knew I had to leave the building at a certain time, and I was crystal clear on what moved the business forward fast and what wouldn't have tremendous impact. How do you say no to bosses, owners, stakeholders, direct reports, and peers? You do so with clarity, kindness, and confidence. When someone asks you to do something that doesn't align with your top goals, explain what you need to spend time on instead and the value of achieving said goal. You can offer support and resources based on your time. Remember, you are in charge of your calendar, and it's up to you to know and stay committed to your priorities.

Why is it that Scandinavians are so happy and have the highest life and work satisfaction? While there are many reasons, one key aspect is their balance between work and leisure activities, including sleep. A Gallup poll found that 14% of American workers are actively disengaged, meaning they are "emotionally disconnected from their workplaces and less likely to be productive." The same poll found that only 10% of Danish workers are emotionally disconnected. While the average American works 1,780 hours and the average South Korean 2,024 hours per year, the average Dane works only 1,408, according to statistics by the Organization for Economic Cooperation and Development (OECD). Danes also have more leisure hours than any other OECD workers, and the link between sufficient leisure and happiness is well-established in OECD's research. Danish companies recognize that employees also have a life outside of work and that working 80 hours a week is bad for both employees and the bottom line.

As mentioned earlier, efficiency increases when you are executing brilliantly. When you are more productive and efficient, you're more successful at work and create a balanced lifestyle for yourself. Happiness stems from making progress in your work in addition to having time for exercise, friends, family, hobbies, and leisure. Balance brings happiness. Your intellectual well-being is activated when you learn from others who've accomplished what you are seeking to do. Research supports how organization brings us inner calm and peace. Taking the time to stay organized each day and week enables you to focus on your top priorities and lowers your stress and anxiety, making you happy.

Focus supports you in executing brilliantly. Neuroscience has proven that we can train our brain for attention with consistent meditation and by turning off all digital notifications, closing down our email when we are working, and resisting the distracting impulses.

Intermittent fasting also improves connectivity in our brains with neuron growth and maintenance.[17] Neuroscience also demonstrates that there's no such thing as multitasking in the brain. What is actually occurring is very fast task-switching. Evidence-based strategies to improve focus and attention include meditation, exercise, hydration, listening to classical music, drinking tea, playing a musical instrument, and chess training.

How would you rate your execution at work today? Is there room for improvement? I know that fast and accurate execution is one of my strengths, and I want it to be one of yours as well. Brilliant execution requires focus, organization, commitment, planning, and, most of all, the right mindset. When you create the right plans and operate with the right boundaries, you can have an incredibly happy and balanced life. I am here as your guide and your partner. I want you to succeed and enjoy every single step of the journey!

Happy Leader Prompts

1. Write down the top five goals for your position. They should be concise and clear. Place them in a location at work where you see them daily.
2. Choose a simple tool to create PLANS quickly for yourself and your team. Utilize this tool each time that you have a business objective.
3. What is one area where you want to grow professionally? Find someone who is excellent at this, and either hire them or be mentored by them.

CHAPTER 9:

Step Four—Prioritize Relationships Over To-Do Lists

t was around 7:00 P.M. on a Tuesday night at the W Court Hotel in New York City. The office was completely dark except for the lights at my cubicle and Jessica's on the other side of the room. My feet hurt from wearing my high heels all day, and my eyes were tired. The office was so quiet that I could hear her typing on her keyboard from across the room. I had been in my associate director position for a few months now and had connected and built relationships with the entire team, except for Jessica. She was very experienced in the New York market, where I was brand-new. She knew her sales market inside and out and reported to me and another person due to the business type. Jessica was intelligent, sassy, and had the opposite of a warm and fuzzy personality. I had made an effort to get to know her and her position but received a polite yet cold response; she wasn't interested in getting close to me.

I stopped typing on my computer and rested my hands on my lap. "I need to just walk over there and connect with her," I thought to myself. I took off my heels and slipped on some comfortable flat shoes. I stood up and stretched and walked over to her side of the large office. I grabbed a chair from someone else's cubicle and pulled it up next to her. She stopped typing and slowly turned her chair around to face me in the small dimly lit space. Her energy was big and questioning, as if to say, "What is so important right now that you need to come and stop me and my work?"

"I know you are busy; I am, too. I wanted to come over here and just get to know you."

"Get to know me?" she asked with disbelief and a bit of snark.

"Yes, I do. We spend a lot of time working together, and I want you to know me as well. I know you used to live in San Francisco. What made you make the move to New York?"

She paused for a long time and then slowly smiled. "I have always had a dream of working in Manhattan, and I had to make it come true."

"Me too! I felt the exact same way."

"What was it like moving from Kauai to New York? What a change!" she asked me.

We proceeded to talk for two hours straight late into the night. From that point onward, she was my ally and supporter. While the other departmental directors felt as if she could not be "managed," we were partners. Not only did getting to know her closely help me as a leader, but she also taught me in a very quick time span all about her market, which was very valuable for me at that time. Jessica became my raving fan, voicing to my boss's boss and all the general managers how strong and effective I was. She became my supporter, and I learned how to lead and inspire a very large and difficult personality. Are you currently leading people that have a very different personality than your own?

When you start a new leadership position, I want you to ask yourself these questions:

- Who are these people that I am leading?
- Who are these people that are my peers and stakeholders?

You want to get to know and really understand your direct reports as individuals. Understand their personality, backgrounds, strengths, and weaknesses. You want to know the specifics of their short- and long-term goals and aspirations, not just for their career, but for their life. Ask them about their perspective on the team, the company, the competitors, and the opportunities. Have them tell you about any threats that they see. Ask what motivates them and what type of communication works the best for them. Learn how to specifically inspire and motivate each of them.

I honestly believe that the stakeholder relationship, described below, is one of the most important relationships you can have as a leader. When you are beginning your career, you are building up experience, knowledge, and confidence about your industry and position. I was lucky in that I had several bosses who were extremely talented when it came to communicating with upper management, and I learned quickly from them.

Know and Manage the Stakeholders

Whenever you start a new position, be extremely curious about exactly who in the organization can influence your team for the better or worse. This is very important! As a leader, it is your responsibility to support your team members and remove as many obstacles as possible that are in their way. You are responsible for creating an environment and team that will allow them to be successful. Your peers and stakeholders have the ability to make decisions that can negatively affect your team. You need to know who these people are, build positive relationships with them, and be able to influence them.

Throughout my career, I worked with some very difficult stakeholders. Connecting with them was one of my strengths. There were instances when stakeholders communicated directly with my team and direct reports, creating havoc in our team culture. In response, I built an organizational chart in my mind and on my computer about whose motives and decisions affected my team. You want to know who they are, exactly what they do, and how much influence they have on your area. Understand their relationships with your boss and peers. Your goal is to build professional and personal relationships with every stakeholder that can and does affect your team.

Think of yourself as the protector and gatekeeper of your team. You want all stakeholders to know you and come to you, not your team, with questions and information. Of course, your team can have relationships with the stakeholders, which can help them grow and even get promoted. Your goal is to have close relationships with the stakeholders.

It's imperative that you buffer very negative news from the stakeholders and protect your team's energy and motivation. It doesn't mean that you hide from your team what's going on, but you might need to change how the information is delivered to them. When I received negative information from a stakeholder, I took time to process it alone. Then, I created an action plan prior to dispersing the news to my team members, where I communicated the challenge, along with the possibilities. You are responsible for the energy of your team, and you don't want any stakeholder chaos and stress trickling down to them.

Set boundaries on what you will and will not do. Know if a stakeholder request aligns with your big, important goals and with the direction you want to go in. Be able to speak with clarity about it. Always communicate with respect and curiosity but know when to speak up. You might have stakeholders, and I absolutely did, that wanted to suck up half your time with their work and projects. Learn how to communicate that their requests will not move you towards your goals and that your plan is to beat all of their targets. Have the confidence and knowledge to disagree with certain items that you are passionate about with your boss, peers, and stakeholders in meetings. Stakeholders and business owners will respect your views and passion, and it will add to your credibility.

Back when my husband and I were both working at the W Istanbul Hotel together, he was the general manager, and I was the director of marketing and public relations. The hotel hadn't been performing well, and my husband's goal was to turn the property around. One of the finance executives in the ownership group focused entirely on cost-cutting initiatives and questioned every single expense. My husband clearly and articulately explained what needed to be invested in so that the hotel could make more money and increase its profit margin. He understood the owner's goals of making more money and showed this executive exactly how to do so. People in different positions above you do not have the perspective and experience that you do.

Everyone Is Coachable

Never judge a person prior to getting to know them. Really get to know them, including their life story and their whole being. Approach each person with curiosity and kindness. It may be difficult to do at times, but you must remove all judgment and learn how to catch yourself judging people on your team. You can do this by slowing down and noticing when you have a negative or judgmental thought about another person. Pause, journal, and reflect on these thoughts and be curious as to where they are coming from. You can also talk to a trusted friend, family member, or peer about the judgmental thoughts and ask for more perspectives. These judgments may stem from your past experiences or upbringing, and it's crucial as a leader that you approach each person on your team with openness. Believe that every single person can and will grow and change, and you will also! You'll learn the most from those who are the complete opposite of you.

Know that every single person, including you, has the ability to change. As a certified coach with the International Coaching Federation, I fully believe in the power of coaching. I have seen transformation happen in my own life, and in the lives of others as well, due to coaching. You don't need to be certified in this area, but I highly recommend that you read books about coaching and understand how to coach people well. Coaches believe that people have the answers inside of them. As a leader, you are their partner, there to ensure they are completely aligned with their goals and intentions. Your direct reports are the ones "steering the ship," and you must ask powerful questions to support them in having new awareness and insight. As a coaching leader, you must hold them accountable and ensure they are making commitments to themselves and to you.

Ensure Each Person Feels Appreciated

Do you feel honored that you get to lead this group of people? I met with my direct reports every other week, and I never canceled our one-on-one meetings. These meetings were theirs, and they thanked me for prioritizing them. Yes, I had a to-do list a mile long, and I absolutely wanted to cancel these meetings at times, especially when the owners or my boss had pressing work that I needed to finish. But I didn't because I knew how important it was for everyone to feel heard. Early in my career, I canceled a few of these employee-centric meetings, and I noticed their nonverbal reactions. They were bothered. Be committed to the time with your team and remember that they are your priority.

Always have your door open and be available to each person on your team. Remember that you are there for them, so show them that you truly care. Learn each person's strengths, weaknesses, challenges, frustrations, dreams, and ideas right away. You want them to know that you are shoulder to shoulder with them, there to lift them up and hold them accountable. My team members always knew that I had their back 150 percent.

Be attuned to their small and large successes and the progress that they are making along the way. Motivational speaker Tony Robbins says that happiness is progress. As a leader, it's your responsibility to appreciate your team members as people and to recognize the progress they are making in their work. You can do this via email, a meeting, or a handwritten card, or by giving them a small gift that aligns with their personality. Small moments of continuous appreciation will fuel them to keep working with dedication and passion. I always celebrated when my team members had massive successes, and the entire team (and sometimes other departments) would join in on the celebration. Be their coach and their guide. Show up every single day being authentic for them.

Acceptance

Leading people is not simple or easy. Human beings are complicated and messy, and leadership is a privilege and challenging. I believe that the difficult parts about being a leader isn't the work itself. It's when you're stretched and tested with the various aspects of people and situations. The path to becoming a happy and healthy leader isn't always calm and stress-free. You will get stronger and wiser as you go, however, building up a toolbox of strategies that you can return to during tough times. There are sunny skies and there are storms—this is leadership.

Accept that you are consistently growing and changing. Self-awareness is as important as the knowledge and experience that you have. Acknowledge your shortcomings and weaknesses and even be up front about them to your boss, peers, and your direct reports. Get support from inside or outside of the organization where you are being extremely challenged emotionally and intellectually. Support can come from friends, family, or other like-minded professionals. You are on a journey; be proud of who you are and who you are becoming.

In addition, be aware of your emotions at all times. Emotional intelligence is not only effective but required in today's business world. Learn how to manage your emotions at work in healthy and productive ways and have stress outlets in your daily and weekly routines. Exercise, meditation, journaling, and spending time with friends and family are all examples. You must know when you need to walk away from a conversation before you lose control. I learned over the years to not take anything personally. It's work; it's not you. I used to be so connected to my job, title, the organization, and my reputation. Remember, you are *not* your job! You are a human being who is doing a job.

One Thursday night, I was driving home from the W Hollywood. It was warm, and my upper back was in excruciating pain. It held all of the tension of the day, the week, and the last three months at the job. My mind raced with a million thoughts about all the things I needed to do, that I had done, and that I hadn't done. The mental load overwhelmed me. I was hungry, as I hadn't eaten since noon that day, and my mouth was terribly dry. My heart raced, and I felt myself taking short, shallow breaths.

I parked in my apartment building garage and sat in my car reflecting on my thoughts and emotions. "I am failing, I am failing," I thought. "I am not going to succeed. I cannot do this. I am not good enough. They were right. I should not have taken this job. What will I do? I don't know if I can do this. I am not good enough. It is killing me."

I sat there for a very long time, breathing heavily, connecting to my thoughts, my physical body, and my feelings. I sat there until my breath slowed and became rhythmic. At last, my mind cleared.

"They are *so* lucky to have me," I thought. "Either I need to make this job work for me, or I need to leave. There are tons of hotels all over Los Angeles that would love to have me. There's no reason to be filled with this much stress and anxiety. Either I make the job work for myself, or I go find a new job."

I decided to meet with my boss, Leon, the next day to tell him what needed to change in order for the sales and marketing team to be successful. First thing the following morning, I had an honest and direct conversation with Leon about the stakeholders and how suffocated I felt. He listened closely, asked clarifying questions and, within a day, made the necessary changes to improve my work experience and the volume of communication from the owners. Going into the meeting, I didn't know what the outcome would be. What I did know, however, was that something needed to change and that I was the only one who could communicate my needs. Be confident about what you need to be successful, and then be fearless when it comes to communicating that with your boss. You were hired for a reason, and they need your passion, intellect, and clarity!

You can absolutely have connected and strong relationships with every person on your team and the stakeholders. You can operate with confidence and calm. Your relationships and your network are some of the most valuable assets that you have as a professional and as a person. Be excited about each position and know that you can climb every single mountain in front of you! You are partnering with and leading people, and it's one of the very best parts of the job.

Healthy relationships at work are crucial for happiness at work and impact how happy you are outside of work as well. When you are in a leadership position, you're responsible for connecting with your team, colleagues, and the stakeholders on a personal level. Utilizing coaching in leadership enables you to motivate your team members and create a culture of accountability and passion. Empowering them will make you happier, as you won't need to micromanage them and stay on top of every single project and task. When your team members flourish, you flourish. You will feel happy when they genuinely feel appreciated and supported by you. Believe in yourself, and communicate with confidence to your team, boss, and the stakeholders. Your happiness will soar as you lift up the people around you.

Are you ready to learn about your number one priority? Now we will turn to do just that in the next chapter.

Happy Leader Prompts

1. Make a list of everyone you lead, each of your peers, and your key stakeholders. Highlight the names of the people with whom there is opportunity to build stronger personal and professional relationships. Schedule time in your calendar to accomplish this.

2. Educate yourself on how to improve your coaching skills. Take a class, read books, and watch videos.

3. At the beginning of each month, set a time in your calendar to decide how you will show appreciation to your team and your individual direct reports.

CHAPTER 10:

Step Five—Your Number One Priority

The director of human resources and I were sitting in the small, windowless meeting room in the building's basement. The buzzing sound of the room's electric lights was annoying and way too loud. My hands rested on the table on top of suspension paperwork. The director sat next to me on the same side of the table in silence. My legs were crossed and shaking. I couldn't stop moving them if I wanted to. My mouth felt so dry that I was cursing myself for forgetting to bring in my water. I felt nervous and uncomfortable, unsure of how this meeting would go. I knew it was the right decision and wasn't looking forward to the conversation. We were about to suspend a director, who reported to me, for several reasons. This particular director had a very strong personality, and I was preparing myself for a difficult conversation.

The director who reported to me walked into the room. She stood next to the table, glaring down at us with her arms crossed. Her presence and energy were strong.

"Clair, please sit down," I said. It took all of my being to not let the tremble inside of me reverberate in my voice. She looked at me, not saying a word. Finally, she sat directly across from me and glared. She didn't even blink.

I slowly turned over the suspension paperwork and held it in front of me. Taking slow breaths, I planted both of my high heels on the ground beneath the table for stability.

I started to read the employee suspension statement to the director that we were terminating.

As I was reading, I felt her anger towards me growing. I glanced up as I read through the entire document, and she continued to glare at me. She didn't speak, but her look said everything I needed to know. I finally read the last sentence: "You are suspended immediately with pending termination."

"What!" she screamed and stood up out of her chair. "This is crazy! You are wrong. I am one of the best in the industry! You will be sorry for this, Tia!"

She advanced closer to me around the table, and my heart began to race. The thought of her punching me flashed through my mind. The director of human resources stood up and stated, "Clair, I will escort you to your office to collect your things now."

Clair did not take her eyes off of me. If fire could have shot out of her pupils, it would have burned me alive. She then turned abruptly and snatched opened the door. Stress pumped through my body and mind. As soon as they both walked out, I exhaled. It was done.

The previous story is about holding someone accountable. Your number one priority as a leader is your team members and the group as a whole, your team. I'm going to share with you exactly how I've led my teams, which created incredible results. In my current position, I am the founder, an inspirationist, and chief happiness officer at Arrive At Happy. As you know, I teach others how to increase their well-being and create incredible work cultures and environments through people.

Active Whole-Being Listening

We live in an age of distraction. Email, text, social media, phone calls, the news, etc., are fighting for our attention every second of the day. Being able to focus and listen with your ears, body, intuition, and whole being takes effort and focus. When one of my direct reports or anyone from the organization comes to speak to me in my office, I close the door and create a quiet space. I turn my body away from my keyboard and computer screen and either face them from across the desk, or I get up and sit next to them. I hold my notebook and pen in my hands, and my body is facing them. My body language communicates openness and support to hold the energy of the conversation. I listen, take notes, and ask open-ended clarifying questions of them.

Rarely do people have the opportunity to be heard. Active whole-being listening takes intention and effort. As a leader, you want the other person to feel *really* heard. This type of listening occurs when you use your entire body. It creates a bond and trust and moves the individual and team forward. The idea is not to listen and then jump in with all of your ideas and suggestions. You want to partner with them in order to gain new insights and communicate solution ideas.

Rick Fulwiler, ScD, teaches management and leadership skills for environmental health and safety professionals at the Harvard T.H. Chan School of Public Health. "Effective listening," according to Dr. Fulwiler, "is a critical component of being a transformational leader, in which you focus on not just the task but also the person doing the work. This type of leadership is more likely to inspire excellence and dedication from your employees than if you only care about their output."[18]

Consistency and Fairness

Being consistent and fair with your team creates a strong foundation. Most likely, you are leading a variety of personalities, which isn't always easy, but it is important. Fairness is an important value that can strengthen the team. Routines and rhythms are comforting to people. I met with my entire team every single month and never missed a month. The meetings were motivational, educational, and tied to the short- and long-term goals. Every single person was required to attend and expected to contribute. This consistent team gathering moves the business forward, incorporating a 100 percent investment in them. I am always shocked when I hear about other leaders going months without holding team meetings.

Ask for direct feedback from every person on your team, in addition to your boss and peers. I am always curious about how people think I'm doing and what they're feeling. I'm not waiting for an annual survey to know the sentiment of my team. Ask them what they feel you can improve upon and how your communication style is being interpreted, and about their ideas on how to improve work, the team, and the office environment. Check in with your boss to get feedback from him as well.

There are benefits to focusing on people's strengths and this directly connects to their professional success. In a study of nearly 10,000 New Zealand workers that examined indicators of flourishing, workers who reported a high awareness of their strengths were 9.5 times more likely to be flourishing than those with low strengths awareness.[19] Moreover, workers who reported high strengths use were 18 times more likely to be flourishing than those with low strengths use.

Meet with every person every other week to discuss their strategies, tactics, and how you can support them. You want to consistently use coaching and accountability to stand shoulder to shoulder with them. Whether you're working virtually or in an office, check in with people daily by asking them about their weekend, their projects, and how things are going in general. While it doesn't take a lot of time, a majority of leaders actually don't make this their top priority.

Give direct, constructive feedback to each of your team members when it's required. If you're a newer leader, it might be uncomfortable for both people involved. However uncomfortable, the goal is to provide the team member with this feedback within 24 hours of the person's action. Use the following style of communication, which I've successfully used for years. First, ask them about the event and actively listen and take notes. Then, when you are speaking to them, focus on their specific behaviors and not on them as a person. Communicate the effect of their negative behavior, the desired positive behavior, and the reason for the desired behavior. I would share that you know they can grow and that you believe in them. Then, give them time and space to talk, and, again, take notes. Consistently follow your organization's human resource guidelines for progressive discipline, verbal, written, etc. Move people out of positions (and the company if necessary) if their work and behavior don't successfully meet their job requirements. One of the largest factors that can hurt a team and performance is not utilizing progressive discipline effectively and not removing people when they are not performing.

Timely Communication

Accurate and timely communication is an area where leaders often struggle. I want you to excel in this area as I did, and this is how I did so. I would receive information from the stakeholders, my peers, or my boss, and then I would immediately communicate the information to my team via email or in person, either that day or at the latest within 24 hours of receiving the information. Understand what is pertinent and helpful to them. You don't want your team to receive information late, from someone else, or not receive it at all. You must deliver every piece of information that you can to help them be successful. Sit down at your desk and write out a quick email with bullet points. Reemphasize that information in person or over the phone when you need to triple-check that they received it. I've always found it easier and more effective to communicate quickly and with simplicity. You don't want your team saying, "I didn't know." Make timely communication a principle for yourself and commit to it daily.

Encouragement Through Teaching

Do you really enjoy teaching others? Are you making time to teach regularly? You can teach in many different ways as a leader. Bring together your entire group and ask what topics and knowledge they would like to learn. Teach them about information that's being discussed at the executive and ownership levels, for example. My suggestion is to discuss a combination of personal development and industry-specific information for personal and professional growth. Teach in both small groups and individually. I always receive consistent positive feedback about how my teams appreciated the time I took to teach them. Remember, when your team members are happy and motivated, they will be more productive, engaged, creative, and effective. Your job is to boost them up and to show them that you believe in them.

One area of positive psychology that I always teach to leaders is intellectual well-being. I learned a variety of intellectual well-being topics from the positive psychology courses through the Happiness Studies Academy. As I've previously stated, one key point to remember is that adults thrive and are happier when they are learning. As a leader, you can share TED Talks and personal development books and lead workshop days when you and your teams are stretching and growing versus working "in the business." Support their taking classes and share the learning resources that have enabled you to get to where you are.

Every Leader Is a Human Resource Leader

I want you to always remember that you are part of a human resource (HR) team. You will struggle and face ongoing challenges if you leave all of the HR work up to your company's people team. Think of an HR team as your partner and resource, not simply people to whom you delegate work. It's my belief and experience that leaders must be actively recruiting as soon as a position is open. Your people are your number one priority, and it's your responsibility to assemble the best people to work with you. Invite your counterparts from all over the city or your area to meet in person or virtually and build relationships with them. Knowing and connecting with those who are doing your job for other companies is one of the best tactics to use in order to learn more about your job. My counterparts and I also support each other when it comes to recruitment. In his book, *Delivering Happiness,* Zappos founding CEO Tony Hsieh says that your people are not your biggest asset, your pipeline is. This is so true. Even if no one is leaving your team right now, you should always have a list of great candidates that you could potentially recruit.

Your goal is to build a reputation for being an amazing leader, having a phenomenal team, and helping build a great place to work. I've always known that the directors who reported to me were consistently talking to their counterparts around the city and country. I always want them to say, "Tia is the best!" My goal was to promote people internally as often as I could. Being able to promote from within an organization is one of the best aspects of being a leader! You have the ability to positively impact people's lives and affect the trajectory of their careers.

I was always shocked and sad when someone on my team told me they were leaving because they were moving, changing industries, etc. Very rarely did I have people leave to go to work for the competition, for more money, or for a better title.

Team members leave managers. If members of your team are leaving, you need to take a long, hard look at yourself and see it as an opportunity to improve. Whenever someone left my team, my priorities immediately shifted. My number one focus was to find a new team member. I moved into hyper-recruiting mode and became a networking master on LinkedIn. My goal was to reach out to as many qualified candidates as possible and to set up interviews within days of someone resigning. The owners, my boss, and my peers were in awe of how fast I would fill my open positions with quality candidates. Your goal is to create relationships and an environment where people don't want to leave. However, if they do for various external reasons, you must prioritize recruiting and engage in it with passion and persistence.

The Small Things Really Matter

As you know I had the great fortune to work at luxury hotels in Hawaii, New York, Istanbul, and Los Angeles. While the properties and grounds were always stunning, my team's offices were not. Hotels find whatever space is left over in the building and turn them into cramped tiny offices for the administrative and sales departments. In Istanbul, I sat in an open rectangular black room with eight other people. It was literally a long, small room with dark carpet, black walls, and a black ceiling. I found myself wondering why anyone would paint an office black. Tables and chairs were placed around the perimeter of the room, and the office was loud. That office was probably the worst I have experienced in my career.

It's your responsibility to create a positive work environment for your team to the best of your ability. While I wasn't able to add windows and give each team member in that dark office a gorgeous space of their own, I focused on what I could do. Show your team that you care and that you are putting in effort. Think of their office space as your second home. If all (or part) of your team is working from home, think of how you can support them in making their workspace in their home positive and inspirational. Ideas for traditional office spaces or working from home include providing them with plants, stand-up desks, healthy snacks, pictures, lighting, a great coffee machine, and a water cooler. One of my teams and I stayed after work one evening and together painted an accent wall in our office. Continuously ask your team for their suggestions about bettering their environment, and work to execute what you can.

"Primers" are words in your physical environment, and they can support you in increasing your happiness and your success. I learned about primers from Dr. Ben-Shahar at the Happiness

Studies Academy. Think of a word or phrase that embodies the mission of your team and put that word on their office wall. Let's say you are a creative team. You could hang a sign that says, "Endless Possibilities!" If you want more peace and serenity in your home life, you could hang a sign that reads "CALM" in your bathroom, for example.

Foster Appropriate Friendships

While it may seem counterintuitive to you, I wholeheartedly believe in fostering friendships. Friendships among people on your team support an organization's goals. In the Gallup Q12 Engagement Survey, the number one question that predicts the success and profitability at a company is "Do you have a best friend at work?" Your goal is to have everyone on your team(s) feel connected and cared for, and to have a sense of belonging. When I was certified as a chief happiness officer in Denmark, we spent a significant amount of time learning about the benefits of having people feel like they belong, not because of their job description and work contribution, but because they are a human being. It is your responsibility to manage the team's relationships effectively and to be aware of anyone feeling left out.

One important thing to remember is that you are not their friend or coworker; you are their boss. You might need to have progressive discipline and likely will have hard conversations. Keep these distinctions clear.

Here are some different ways that you can foster friendships on your team. Enjoy a potluck together, do an escape room, go bowling, have a picnic, and or even take part in a drum circle! In my monthly team meeting, I always ask everyone for ideas of experiences that we could do together as a team, and then they would vote anonymously. Usually, when I would start a new leadership position, no money was available for team outings in the budget. However, I would find money from another line and reallocate it towards team outings. You don't need to spend a lot, and often you can barter with companies for outings or even just gather your team at your home with a bit of food and wine. For example, I placed "Wednesday Walks" on my team's calendar, when, as a team, we gathered to walk for 30 minutes every week. We all enjoyed the fresh air, movement, and connection! Plus, it was free! I also added a weekly event in their team calendar and titled it "Celebrate!" At 5 p.m. every Friday we gathered in a circle and each person said one thing that they were celebrating, either personally or professionally, that week.

One of my team members launched a "Fairy Godmother" program. (You can rename this, of course!) In this program, every person filled out a form answering questions about themselves. Each team member became a "fairy godmother" to someone else and surprised them on their work anniversary, birthday, or for no reason in particular. Also, the fairy godmother usually knew when their person was going through a challenge and delighted them with a personalized surprise. Who doesn't need a fairy godmother in their life? You can leave little notes of appreciation for something specific either on a team member's monitor or mail cards to them. Interdepartmental friendships strengthen an organization. Organize ways to surprise and appreciate other teams. Foster friendships between team members and watch them blossom.

Know Thyself with Constant Evolution

Do you know your strengths? Are you able to name your top three right now? How well do you know your weaknesses? Self-awareness is knowing your personality traits, your behaviors, and what triggers you. It's the ability to have a crystal clear, objective view of yourself and to recognize patterns. Through feedback from people that I worked with and for, as well as several personality tests, I clarified my strengths and weaknesses, which enabled me to lead effectively and authentically. I was always very transparent about my personality and would apologize quickly and publicly when I made mistakes. My advice to you is to show your team that you are human.

Self-management is taking responsibility for one's own behavior and well-being. Your work and your life will challenge you and throw curveballs. It's your duty to separate yourself from the events and circumstances in your life and choose how you want to respond. Earlier in my career, I would be angry at a situation at work, and my team would see my anger come out in nonprofessional ways at times. I learned over the years that I could share and show my emotions in a productive and healthy way. How you do this is to increase your emotional granularity (the number of emotions that you know and recognize); understand that emotions are created from your past experiences, the physical sensations in your body, and your predictions; label your emotions or reframe them; communicate by talking or journaling when you are going through challenges; and slow down before reacting. Give yourself time to process and reflect before acting. Once you know how to do this, you can be a coach and guide for your team and peers. This is a very challenging aspect of professional life for some people, and it takes focus and attention.

Take constructive feedback from people very seriously. Create daily and weekly rituals as well as a plan to change and grow from the feedback that you are given. Have people in your life that you can learn from and talk to about the challenges that you go through at work. They can be friends, family, a therapist or coach, or anyone else who can listen and provide helpful perspective and new insights. We don't learn from experience; we learn and grow from reflecting about our experience.

I previously mentioned the concept of "ReflAction." On a regular basis, make space for reflection through meditation, journaling, spending time with Mother Nature, or talking with others. After this reflection period, you can then act and move forward again. Take what you have learned and apply it to how you lead and work. Per Dr. Ben-Shahar, many of us are moving too fast. He has shared the dangers of moving so fast and not taking the time to pause and reflect on an ongoing basis.

Neuroplasticity, the study of how the brain can structurally and functionally rewire itself as a result of experience, has been studied for the past 50 years. All experiences alter the brain and can lead to small-scale or large-scale changes. If you meditate consistently for 10 minutes a day for 8 weeks straight, your brain will physically change, and you will be calmer and more resilient.[20] The amazing fact is that we are never stuck! Repetition is the foundation of neuroplasticity, and the more repetition you have with an experience, the more change will occur in your brain. Our brains are not infinitely plastic, per Dr. O'Brien from The Neuroscience School. She teaches that limits on neuroplasticity include our genes, cognitive ability, personality, and physical traits. It's interesting to note that both habits and habitual thoughts will create structural and functional brain change, for the better and for the worse. Here are some evidence-based ideas for a more flexible brain! Intermittent fasting, travel, learning a new language or musical instrument, using your nondominant hand, expanding your vocabulary, creating artwork, dancing, and sleep. Know yourself and commit to always evolving and becoming a better version of yourself for the people you lead.

Psychological Safety

Do you know what makes a team truly successful? What creates high performance, innovation, and outstanding productivity?

In 2012, Google's People Analytics team went on a quest to find what makes the perfect team.[21] They spent years analyzing people, work output, and how teams work together. Named "Project Aristotle," this study researched a half-century of academic studies looking at how teams worked. What they discovered was surprising. The "who" part of the team equation didn't seem to matter. The analytics team kept coming upon research known as "group norms." Group norms are the traditions, behavioral standards, and unwritten rules that govern how we function when we gather.

What the research concluded was that how teammates treated each other distinguished good teams from mediocre teams or bad teams. There were two behaviors that all good teams generally shared. First, members of the team spoke in roughly the same proportion. No one person was overpowering or dominating. Second, team members were intuitive and knew how others were feeling based on nonverbal communication. Members could tell based on their tone of voice, their expressions, and other cues how people were feeling. Amy Edmondson, a Harvard Business School professor, defines "psychological safety" as a "shared belief held by members of a team that the team is safe for interpersonal risk-taking." Project Aristotle demonstrated that people want to be treated equally at work and need their peers to respect them. People at work also need to be closely connected so that colleagues know when they are going through emotional challenges.

To create an environment that is psychologically safe, leaders must create an environment where people truly care about one another. Team members must know enough about their colleague's personal lives to be able to read nonverbal cues and to be there to support their team members in times of need. People must care about and respect one another so they feel that they can make themselves vulnerable and share all ideas without getting shut down. Even though there may be a hierarchical structure in the team, all team members should contribute in ongoing meaningful ways. One of the dynamics you might observe in psychologically safe teams would be a good degree of banter, the playful and friendly exchange of teasing remarks, or small talk at the beginning of meetings.

Your daily happiness will increase when you are fully engaged and connected to your team. Creating an environment with connected relationships will enable everyone to flourish emotionally and psychologically. When you learn and engage in active listening, you are more effective at communicating and creating a culture of trust and authenticity. You will feel a sense of calm during chaotic times because you will know the power of whole-being listening and human understanding. Being consistent, fair, and timely will enable you to retain the best talent and be thankful that you aren't constantly having to recruit new members for your teams. Always prioritizing self-awareness, self-discovery, and self-management will increase your happiness because you are growing and evolving for the better.

I believe that leading other people successfully is one of the hardest jobs, yet one of the most rewarding. Remember that your people truly are your number one priority, and they need you to lead them with positivity and support. Always remember that you have resources to help you and that you are never alone. When you prioritize your team members and your team as a whole, you will be successful. A working rhythm and team culture is created when the group has psychological safety. I absolutely believe that you can implement all of these elements into your leadership style and that doing so will make work fun. This book has covered six out of the eight steps, and you're on your way to elevating your happiness and effectiveness! Keep in mind the life and positions that you want in the future, and trust that you can be whoever you want to be.

Happy Leader Prompts

1. Commit to Active Whole-Being Listening and place a physical reminder in your work area of this intention.
2. Ask your direct reports and boss about how consistent and fair they feel you are. Take their feedback to heart and ask for suggestions on how to improve.
3. Complete a Strengths-Finder report with your team, and have each person commit to using their top-three strengths in specific ways at work.

CHAPTER 11:
Step Six—Measure to Excel

I was sitting in my boss's office at The Westin Princeville Ocean Resort Villas on the north shore of the island of Kauai, Hawaii. It was 9:00 A.M., and I had just driven for an hour up the island from my basement suite on the south shore. Her office was spotless and overlooked the Porte cochere. The hotel had recently opened, and 30 percent of the project was still under construction. You could see the dirt patches and construction piles throughout the landscaping and hear the sound of small Bobcats working around the property. I felt awake and energized, having completed my usual 60-minute walk up the steep hill next to my home and downed my Starbucks coffee during the drive. I always loved driving to this new property and was excited and honored that I was the opening director of sales and marketing. I spent every Friday at this hotel and every Monday through Thursday on the south shore at the Sheraton Kauai Resort. My boss was sitting across from me in her black leather chair, typing on her keyboard. She was wearing her usual navy-blue pantsuit and white shirt. My notebook and pen were at the ready in my lap, and I was curious about what she wanted to discuss. She stopped typing and looked me directly in the eyes.

"Tia, I am very frustrated and confused. We have followed regional's direction and strategies, and the results are just not there. I went to the mainland and hosted numerous client events in our key feeder markets, and the clients still aren't booking. We've spent funds on targeted marketing, and the demand has simply not grown. We established partnership agreements with all the major wholesale customer accounts, and room nights are not picking up. What's going on? Why are we not making sales?"

I answered, "I understand your concerns and thank you for setting up this meeting to discuss them. We are a brand-new property, and one of the only hotels in Hawaii that doesn't have a beach. The property is still under construction, and it will take time. I am confident, though, that business will come."

"Well, we budgeted it to be coming now. We need progress, and we need revenue. I need to know your plan."

"Absolutely. I will connect with the regional team today and have an updated plan for you by Monday morning."

"I appreciate that. We cannot sit empty like this any longer. We need leisure guests into the property for revenue so the vacation ownership team can start to execute against their targets."

"Yes, of course." I stood up and walked out of her office to my cubicle near the window. I sat there thinking, "I know we have performed all the right tactics, and it will just take time." I also knew that I didn't have any more time and needed to make things happen faster. The problem was, I felt we were doing everything right, but we weren't consistent, focused, and were not measuring our tactics daily and weekly. At this point in my leadership career, I wasn't measuring to excel. "Measuring to excel" means you and your team consistently focus on the one main goal and are measuring and completing actions weekly to guarantee that you arrive at that goal.

The concept you must remember forever is:

WHAT GETS MEASURED GETS DONE!

I was first introduced to the book titled *The 4 Disciplines of Execution* by one of my mentors while I was at the W Hollywood Hotel in Los Angeles. I was honestly struggling there to execute my ideas as fast and as well as I needed to. When he gave me the book, my ego was bruised. He didn't say, "You are not doing a great job," but he did say, "Tia, read this book. I think it will help you tremendously."

I remember taking it and sitting back at my desk after he walked away. I was holding the book in my hands and thinking, "How is this business book going to help me?"

He was a mentor and one of my boss's bosses, so I started reading it, of course. I read the majority of it in the front seat of my husband's car on the way to Mammoth Ski Resort, in California, for a weekend ski trip. It was a four-hour drive, and I read half of the book on the way there and the other half on the way back. I took photos of several pages, typing notes into my phone, and underlining, starring, and circling throughout the book. I kept exclaiming, "This book is so good!" "This is amazing!" and "I needed this book eight years ago."

The Four Disciplines of Execution

I arrived at the office at The W Hollywood Hotel on Monday morning full of determination and a newfound energy, ready to launch the Four Disciplines of Execution with my group sales team that day. I brought in a huge new board to use, and I created the "why" around this new system for our team. I was ready to discuss "Wildly Important Goals," a concept from the book. Wildly Important Goals are the two to three most important goals for the team for the year. If a team achieves or beats their Wildly Important Annual Goals, they are viewed as successful.

The four of us had our first Wildly Important Goals (WIGs) meeting that morning, where I definitely received skepticism and uncertain looks and viewed unsure body language. I spoke passionately and with conviction about this new weekly rhythm that we were going to create that would lead us to victory by the year's end. Not only did we meet our goals that year, but we also exceeded them tremendously! The regional vice president that my boss reported to then had me teach and train several of my more experienced colleagues in WIGs. I was successful and even a little famous locally.

The Four Disciplines of Execution is a concept that has been proven in many different industries and team types. Its overarching concept is to have everyone focus on a big goal and communicate and measure their weekly actions.

The Wildly Important Goals

Here is the exact strategy from the book that you can deploy immediately. You and your team first must agree on one main big goal that when achieved or beat will mean success for the group. Together, you must also all agree on the weekly actions that will move the team forward to ensure you win. Without you, your team creates a large whiteboard with date markers on one axis and achievement markers located on the other. This whiteboard can be created physically or created virtually for teams. If the group is in person, the WIG board is hung on the wall in a very visual location so that everyone from the team can see it daily. As the leader, you place a weekly 15-minute meeting titled "WIG Session" in the team's calendar. At this meeting, the board is updated with where the group is relative to the big goal, and each team member speaks about their results from the previous week's key commitments and what three to five actions they are committed to for the current week. These actions consist of what the group has agreed equals success. Accountability is created by the group witnessing each person, and the celebrations are shared. It is energizing and competitive, and it works! You want to continuously talk about results in a positive, motivating, and encouraging way. When the group is falling short in an area, gather to brainstorm, create a plan, and move quickly. I highly recommend implementing the Four Disciplines of Execution if your team isn't exceeding their goals. It is simple, clear, and motivating, and it works!

Empowerment

Your goal as a happy and successful leader is to ensure that each person understands their piece of the larger pie. Empower them to create their own action plans on how they will get there. "Empowering" is creating a culture of trust where you view more in your team members than they see in themselves. As the leader, you are their coach, not the manager. Have your direct reports create their own answers, with you providing new insight, awareness, and accountability. There's more than one way to achieve a goal; there are many ways. Learn from the different ways that your team operates and be humble that your way is certainly not the only way. There is nothing more demotivating than being micromanaged by leaders.

For my Arrive At Happy podcast show, I interviewed Jeff Seltzer, managing director of Hypothesis, a consumer-centric insights, design, and strategy agency. Their clients include companies like Netflix, Disney, and Starbucks. I asked Jeff to describe the culture that contributes to his organization's success:

"We would describe our culture as an empowerment culture. One in which individuals are empowered to make decisions and they have to live with those decisions. They're empowered to create change within the company, to voice new ways of doing things, and new ways of servicing clients. We give people a lot of autonomy and a lot of freedom. We hire people that thrive in an environment that empowers them, and they have to live by the results of their decisions. They have to be the ones that are held accountable. And we've found that, for us, it really works well."

When you feel and know that you are leading your team towards success, you're going to be happier! When you feel that you are making progress in meaningful work, you feel more joy. Having a balanced life with your career, friends and family, health and wellness, and leisure activities increases your life satisfaction. Being crystal clear on your goals with your team also creates alignment and harmony. Instead of goals being stressful, the Four Disciplines of Execution and Wildly Important Goals make accomplishment energetic, competitive, fun, and collaborative! You no longer feel the weight on your shoulders because everyone is moving forward united. There's no better feeling than empowering your team members and watching them soar! Inspiring them through your belief elevates your happiness, guaranteed.

You have now learned how to prioritize and create authentic happiness in your life, the importance of zooming out and seeing the big picture, how to execute fast and brilliantly, leading the whole person, building connected relationships with stakeholders, and knowing your number one priority. All these steps transform the way you live and lead, in addition to elevating your impact on the world. When you master everything that you have read so far in addition to Steps Seven and Eight, you will be happy and an inspirational and wildly successful leader. It takes effort, intention, and healthy daily rituals and reminders, but it's so worth it.

Remember what you stand to gain and the ripple effect that you have the ability to create. I wake up every single day motivated to do my very best, and I truly want the same for you.

Happy Leader Prompts

1. Read the book, *The 4 Disciplines of Execution.*
2. Determine your number one WIG (Wildly Important Goal) with your team.
3. Reflect on how much empowerment you are giving your team right now and write down two strategies that would empower them even more.

CHAPTER 12:

Step Seven—Be the Spark

As the director of sales and marketing at the London West Hollywood at Beverly Hills, I felt I was successfully balancing my career and my personal life. Unless I had a client event at night, I left my office at exactly 5 P.M. and was home by 5:15 to spend the evening with my one daughter and husband. In my personal time, I exercised and spent time with my friends and husband. I had time to relax and overall was getting enough sleep as well. We had a great apartment in West Hollywood, and I was thankful for the warm year-round sunshine. My boss and I were in sync, and I had built an incredibly strong and talented team of sales professionals. My mindset was "I got this!" The hotel had undergone a $40 million renovation and looked incredible.

I remember one once-in-a-lifetime night gathering in the sales office with my team and several of my peers. We had just launched The Penthouse suite, which was inspired by Vivienne Westwood, a famous British fashion designer. The party went until just after midnight and was attended by top clients, celebrities, and the press. The food was world-class, the music unique and energetic, and the vibe was English chic. I was high from the excitement and buzz. I also felt like a million dollars because the Vivienne Westwood team had dressed a few of us, and I was wearing one of the most exquisite dresses I had ever worn. We were all beaming, and the room was filled with pride, joy, connection, and happiness.

"It was incredible!" I shared with my team. "Our clients loved it! The Vivienne Westwood team is super happy as well. You should all feel so proud. All our hard work will definitely pay off! We are going to receive some incredible press coverage!"

Infectious Energy

On a scale of 1 to 10, how energetic are you at work right now? Does your team gain energy from being in your presence, or are you draining them?

Energy is an open-loop circuit, meaning that the vitality you bring to a situation or group will be felt and taken in by the other people around you. Energy is powerful. It can be a positive force in your professional and personal success, and it can be very detrimental. "Emotional contagion" is a well-established phenomenon, where we can take on the emotional states of those surrounding us. It can occur in person and even by watching the news or our social media channels. I had worked extremely hard my entire life, and it was paying off while I was at the London. I've always been an energetic person, and I had a sensation of flow, where I arrived at work every single day to have fun. My team felt empowered, I was motivating the entire hotel, and we were achieving fantastic results. I was consistently receiving 98/100 on my annual reviews.

The owners and the stakeholders were extremely satisfied. I honestly felt like the sky was the limit.

My team and I were in sync and connected. I had a balanced work life, which set an example for the entire team. As their boss, I wasn't sitting in the office until 9 P.M., making everyone feel that they had to do the same. We were efficient and all moving forward together.

Small Wins

The energy I brought to this team (and every team that I lead) was infectious. Acknowledge all that your team has accomplished by continuously sharing the progress the team and the individuals are making. I discovered the book *The Progress Principle* when I was certified as a chief happiness officer in Denmark and getting certified in neuroscience. In the book, the authors, Teresa Amabile and Steven Kramer, explain that employees have an "inner work life." It relates to employees' willpower and motivation. An inner work life consists of a team member's perceptions and thoughts or sense-making about workday events, and often people are unaware of these as they are occurring.[22] It includes both their emotions and feelings—their good and bad moods. Their motivation and drive are another area. These areas influence each other, as it is an inner system of how we feel and behave while working. The book's authors and researchers found that motivation and drive is the primary driver of how people feel about their inner work life.

They explain the "progress loop," which is a concept that every leader must know about and act upon. If I were to ask you, what motivates people at work, would you say progress in meaningful work? The positive form of the progress loop is having forward momentum, which translates into a positive inner work life for a team. Then that positive inner work life translates into more progress, forming an upward spiral. The negative form of the loop is having setbacks, which leads to a negative inner work life, which then leads to more setbacks. As a leader, it's your responsibility to ensure that your team perceives their work as contributing value to something or someone. Dopamine, a neurotransmitter in reward motivation behavior, spikes in anticipation of a reward. It feels good. Recognize those small and simple wins!

Show Up Positive and Optimistic

Your mind and your body are connected. I start my workdays with a great cup of coffee, a healthy breakfast, and exercise, whether that means going for a run, practicing yoga, or going to the gym. I know that my professional success and leadership are connected to the health of my physical body. A lot of research has been done about morning rituals and the right and wrong ways to start your day. Meditation is proven to add calm, patience, and resilience. Look at your mornings and ask yourself, are they setting me up in the right frame of mind to show up positive and optimistic? You must be rested, and you must feel joy and excitement as you start your day of work. Being the spark ignites energy in others and inspires people to do their best work and be the best version of themselves.

When I walk into work, I intentionally bring with me a wave of positive energy. As a leader, you're responsible for how people feel. It is a big responsibility! One way you can start the day positively and with connection is with a "Level Five Good Morning." I learned this term and its meaning during my chief happiness officer certification in Denmark. The Level Five Good Morning is walking up to or by people, looking them in the eye, smiling, and saying good morning! You then ask them something specific about their life or their work or start talking about something going on in the world, and not negative news! I am always shocked when I hear about leaders who don't say good morning to their team members. If you are any type of leader, make your team and other employees in the company feel great as they start their day. If you are leading a virtual team, you can leave short voicemails for people or take three minutes and call them.

Virtual and in-person meetings are a great time to infuse optimism into your team and peers. The directors and managers on my team and I had a weekly meeting with my boss and other executives while I was at the London West Hollywood Hotel. The purpose of the meeting was to update the general manager (my boss) on potential sales opportunities for the hotel. Every week I made it a point to highlight successes from the previous week and to share personal stories of what team members were doing to win. If we had a challenging month but then turned it around, I would congratulate each person who was involved and recognize how they contributed. My praise and focus were on their effort, creativity, tenacity, and teamwork. We also discussed challenges and obstacles as well, but I continually highlighted what was positive and possible for our future.

In her book, *Positivity*, Barbara Fredrickson, PhD, shares several proven methods to increase what she calls "heartfelt positivity." These include finding positive meaning in challenging circumstances, truly savoring the good circumstances and aspects of your life, counting your blessings, kindness, following your passions, dreaming about your future, applying your strengths, connecting with others, and connecting with nature.[23] I encourage you to reflect on how positive you feel daily and weekly, and how you can open your heart and mind to new possibilities.

When you are optimistic, your attitude is hopeful, and you can consider the possibilities of good things happening at work and in life. Optimism is about how we perceive things. Optimistic people are viewed as having both resilience and personal strength. It's not realistic that you or I can be optimistic all of the time. Work and life are challenging and sometimes bring us down psychologically, mentally, and emotionally. Remember that optimism is powerful and is something you can become better at. It will contribute to your success in life and make life more enjoyable to live. Every single one of my bosses over my 15-year career has commented on how much they appreciated my optimistic and positive attitude. On 360-degree review reports, my peers and direct reports would thank me for the same reason. A 360 review is a performance evaluation tool that solicits feedback about an employee from all directions: their managers, coworkers, and direct reports. A 360 review seeks to provide actionable feedback to an employee and gives them a better understanding of their contributions to an organization. An optimistic attitude is to be taken seriously.

Dr. Seligman has written many books, including *Authentic Happiness* and *Learned Optimism*. "Learned optimism" is a concept that states we can change our attitude and behaviors by recognizing and challenging our negative self-talk, among other things. Dr. Seligman teaches that optimism enhances the quality of life and that anyone can learn to practice it. His research proves the incredible effects that optimism has on our lives, which include a strong immune system, motivation and performance, and career success.

You have chosen to lead people and teams, and I want you to be acutely aware that your energy and emotions are contagious. Always remember the mind-body connection and be conscious of when you are feeling off-balance. There are proven evidence-based tactics you can use to increase your levels of positivity and optimism and doing so will directly affect your levels of success in any organization. Be authentic and open with your team when you are having challenging days—you want them to see that you are human, too! Optimism is something you can always become stronger at, and I am on this journey with you.

Positive Communication

Are you truly aware of how you speak and write to your direct reports and colleagues? Communication is one of the most powerful tools that leaders have to either bring people together or hurt relationships. Leaders have countless ways to make others feel better or worse, and it matters. Think about when you are operating at your best, full of energy and hope. How do you talk to your team and family members at these times? What is happening in your life that enables you to show up in this way? Your team cares about their work, and people naturally want to do well. Comment on their strengths, their accomplishments, and their contributions. I share positive news about my team members both publicly and privately.

In his book, *Positive Leadership: Strategies for Extraordinary Performance,* Kim Cameron talks about the power and effects of positive communication on organization success. A study of 60 top-management teams who were involved in strategies, budgets, and problem-solving demonstrated the effects that positive management and communication can have on the organization: "The results of the research revealed that in high-performing organizations, the ratio of positive to negative statements in the top-management teams was 5.6 to 1." In contrast, the low-performing organizations had a ratio of 0.36 to 1. Cameron writes: "Positive statements are those that express appreciation, support, helpfulness, approval, or compliments."[24] The connection between positive communication and business results may not seem intuitive to many leaders. Become aware of how you are communicating, ask for ongoing feedback, and always be open to change and improvement.

Again, be the spark. Take your energy very seriously and choose to bring optimism to work. Know that this is something you can get better at and that you are never stuck. Incredible evidence-based resources from positive psychology can be used to increase your energy, positivity, and optimism. Your teams will be so happy when you are consistently noticing their small wins and congratulating them on making progress and having meaningful work. Being the spark is also about how you show up for your family and friends as well. Many people rely on you, and I know the spark is within you. Have gratitude for all that you have and recognize that there will ups and downs. Be committed to your team, and even when you have those down days, put on your game face and know that by lifting others up, you will lift yourself up as well!

You have almost all my secrets and my full methodology for how to be a wildly successful and happy leader! In the next chapter, I will share exactly how to master your mindset, which is powerful. I truly believe in you and your abilities to grow and be an incredible force in the world. So many people need you to show up, and I am here to support you every step of the way. You got this!

Happy Leader Prompts

1. Take two pieces of paper and draw a line straight down the middle of both. At the top of one paper, write WORK, and at the top of the other, write HOME. Then write ENERGY GAINERS at the top of one column and ENERGY DRAINERS at the top of the other column on each paper, and list as many as you can for both.
2. Read the book *The Progress Principle*.

3. Commit to Optimism and design your personal and professional calendar to align with how you want to feel. Prioritize yourself and your well-being and bring positive energy to work for your team and peers.

CHAPTER 13:
Step Eight—Master Your Mindset

A "mindset" is a set of notions or assumptions held by one person or a group of people. Your mindset at work and in life directly connects to your happiness. Having a positive and optimistic mindset is a choice and is the result of effort and daily habits, or "rituals," as I like to call them. Around the world, there are millions of people who are not happy at work and choose to stay that way. You might be one of these people right now. My intention is to inspire you to create the goal to be really happy at work! I want you to understand how to be a happy and successful leader and to put in the effort to get and stay there. You can absolutely sustain your workplace well-being and be an unbelievable leader! Just think of the possibilities if you master your mindset!

In *Delivering Happiness*, his fantastic book on culture and happiness at work, Tony Hsieh shares his personal and professional stories about his life and the many businesses of which he is a part.

Prior to running Zappos, Hsieh had started a company called LinkExchange with a friend. The company started out small, they hired their friends, and the culture of the company was fun and exciting. As they grew, they made the mistake of hiring people who didn't align with their culture. These new people were interested in money and building their résumés, and going to work at LinkExchange changed, even for the founders.

Hsieh told the story of how one day he woke up for work and hit the snooze button six times. He then realized how much he was dreading going to work, and he wasn't sure what to do. Soon after, Microsoft purchased LinkExchange for $265 million, with a condition that Hsieh and his two colleagues stay on for a minimum of 12 more months. If Hsieh left prior to that time, he would walk away from approximately $8 million. LinkExchange wasn't fun for him anymore. He was successful, wealthy, and had some professional fame. From the outside and to his friends, he had the perfect life and was the very definition of happiness. On the inside, he describes his experience during that time in his life as being on autopilot. He made a list of the happiest periods in life. They included times when he was building, being creative and inventive, and connecting with friends and doing activities that he enjoyed. He thought about how society brainwashed people into thinking that more money and more success equals more happiness. His mindset was that he was wasting his time and wasting his life.

Hsieh chose to do something about his mindset and his experience. He chose to be true to himself, so he walked away from all the money that was keeping him at Microsoft. He didn't know exactly what he was going to do, but he stated he wasn't going to "sit around letting my life and the world pass me by." People thought that he was crazy for giving up so much money and leaving Microsoft. It was a turning point for him and for his life. He "decided to stop chasing money and start chasing the passion." He went on to create and build Zappos.com and became famous for creating the happy culture at the company. Journalists and business leaders from around the world wanted to learn from him and his team about their insane passion for customer happiness! It wasn't an easy road, and there were huge challenges along the way. Hsieh's mindset and mission to live and work for passion changed his life. Zappos was eventually acquired by Amazon in a deal valued at over $1.2 billion. I would absolutely say that he mastered his mindset.

You are in charge of your mindset and how you show up. I discovered that my position and my company were completely independent from who I was. I realized that I was free to do anything that I wanted to do. I was reminded of the power of thoughts and how reframing situations can completely alter your reality. After that realization, I began showing up differently for my work, my family, and myself. I went back to being the conductor of the train of my life, versus being a passenger. I was the driver, and I had always been the driver, but now I chose how I wanted to feel.

Your mindset is the most powerful asset that you have, and it can either hurt or support you. You create your own reality. Two people can be going through the exact same event and perceive it in different ways. Your thoughts inform your emotions, and your emotions inform your thoughts. This chapter gives you potent tools to support you in having a strong and supportive mindset. Master them, along with the other tools we've discussed, and you will truly be unstoppable. Your mindset can bring you inner joy and more happiness.

Self-Development

Consistently brainstorm and think about how you can grow and change. I challenge you to dedicate time with your boss asking about how you can improve. Companies have formal management reviews, but I suggest that you do not wait for these reviews to take place. Be open to feedback, even the feedback that is really hard to hear. If you are making mistakes, it means you are learning. If some new strategies don't work, it means that you are trying. Self-development is about taking control of where you currently are and where you want to be. When you spend time developing yourself at work, it will positively affect your personal life and vice versa.

Seek out incredible resources to help you adapt and stretch yourself. I really enjoy watching TED Talks and reading personal development and business books. The online course world has exploded with content, and you can ask those above you if they can mentor you. I've also worked with consultants, experts, and coaches. Attending conferences has changed my life. I was intro-duced to the number one high-performance coach in the world, Brendon Burchard, by my first coach, and I instantly connected to him and his story. His books, group coaching, and influencer conference have enabled me to grow in exponential ways. You can learn from your peers. I suggest inviting the top leaders in your position to lunch to connect and learn from them.

I believe that, as a leader, it's your responsibility to create an environment for self-development for your team. Find personal-ized and group resources for your team and peers. Initiate book clubs at work and implement new research. I consistently held "class" in my office with one or more of the people from my team, where they could learn about the strategies and expectations of the owners or how to interpret reports, for example. If you are a leader, you are a teacher. Communicate your expectations and excitement for all the learning opportunities available to them! Growing through learning brings about intellectual well-being. You and your team can become happier while learning. Giving and generosity bring happiness. You can be happier by giving your time and energy to helping others grow.

In her *Harvard Business Review* article titled, "The Most Productive Way to Develop as a Leader," Herminia Ibarra asks the question, "What if we didn't see self-development and our notion of self as work and saw it as play instead?" She writes: "Playing with your own notion of yourself is akin to flirting with future possibilities. Like in all forms of play, the journey becomes more important than a pre-set destination."[25] When it comes to areas that you need to improve and grow, I challenge you to move from a place of strategies and planning to one of light and nonjudgmental exploration. You can be more creative, and the process is a lot more fun! Like life, it's not about the destination, but about the meaningful journey.

Open-Mindedness

Throughout my career, my bosses and the owners of the various hotels that I worked for would come to me with new ideas. At times, I thought these ideas were completely insane. My challenge to you is, how can you consistently keep an open mind? For example, when an owner or boss would come to me with a suggestion that was really important to them, I would answer with, "Let's look into this and see how we could do it." It didn't mean that it was guaranteed that we would move forward with it, but it meant that we would try. So much about your success in life is attitude, which is defined as a mental position with regard to a fact or state. Keeping an open mind means you will try new ideas and not shut them down before exploring them. Now, if I did know why a strategy or tactic wouldn't work and had the facts to back it up, I certainly did present those at the beginning. Then I brainstormed with the stakeholder on other ideas. Always have an open mind and a willingness to try new ideas. Always saying yes means being positive and open. When you are positive and open, you are happier inside and a much easier person to work with.

When a large challenge arises at work, what are your thoughts and your emotions? My goal for you is to see obstacles as opportunities in order to move forward. Accept that they are a part of your professional life and be ready for them. When you have built a strong and healthy foundation using Steps One through Seven, you have the physical, psychological, and emotional strength to master your mindset! I suggest you demonstrate this for your teams and walk the talk every single day. Doing so becomes a part of the culture of your teams. Say a large new challenge arises, for example, and you are surprised and thrown off guard. Take the time to understand the problem with questions, reports, and research, but don't take too long. Move quickly from challenge acceptance to acting. Do not "sit" in the challenge very long. The idea is to not be demotivated by the obstacle but to lead your team emotionally as well. Pivoting is a part of life. It means to make a change, a shift, and it means changing directions. Here are some tips on how to keep your team motivated while pivoting. Gather all the data and information you need, make a plan together, and communicate with your team consistently as you are moving through the change. If there is an area in your division that is struggling, turn over every stone to find new solutions and opportunities, and do it with others. Reach out to people who can help you, learn from them, and execute your plan.

Falling Up

One of my favorite science of happiness business books is *The Happiness Advantage* by Harvard's Shawn Achor. His TED Talk on happiness is one of the most popular ever. One of the principles he teaches is "falling up." This is an incredible concept that I have taught to many organizations over the years. "Falling up" is about "capitalizing on the downs to build upward momentum."[26] Achor teaches that there are three mental paths that you can travel when a challenge arises. "The brain is constantly creating and revising mental maps to help us navigate our way through this complex and ever-changing world." The first mental path, or map, keeps us circling where we are, and the second leads us further toward future negative consequences. "The third path leads us from failure or setback to a place where we are stronger and more capable than before the fall." Achor and others call this "post-traumatic growth." Your ability to find the falling-up path is determined by your perception of events, which is the use of acceptance, optimism, and coping mechanisms, and having the ability to positively reinterpret the event. With determination and hard work, you can absolutely be one of the people who, instead of bouncing back, bounces forward!

Bias Towards Innovation

Do you enjoy coming up with new ideas and brainstorming? It's one of my favorite activities to do, and I want it to be the same for you. In all my leadership positions, the expectation was that I had new and creative ideas. My goal for you is to have the mindset, "My team and I are innovative, and we are not stuck in any old ways." Ideas spark ideas and having a bias towards innovation brings energy. Determine the best times and environments for your team to get your creative juices flowing on a consistent basis.

Questions are your very best friend! Ask your teams, bosses, peers, and stakeholders for new ideas all the time.

You can get all sorts of new ideas for your organization from endless resources. Set up Google alerts for all your competitors and key clients, read books and magazines, and research online. Listen closely to what your clients are saying, as they will give you so many new ideas as well.

I found it fascinating to learn about insight during my neuroscience certification. "Insight" is a sudden solution to a long, vexing problem. You can suddenly have a new idea or have a sudden understanding of a complex situation. Five universal stages to insight are available to everyone. The first stage is to explore information in your mind, either by an analytical approach or by engaging in activities that encourage an open mind, like having a new hobby or relaxing in Mother Nature. The second stage is to find and focus on an area that you're passionate about and to develop an expertise through practice and study. The third stage is to incubate the information. You can do so by doing the work, then stepping back, taking breaks, and scheduling downtime. The fourth stage is when you have a new insight. The fifth stage of insight is your follow-through and evaluation of your aha insight moments. Share this information with your team members and evaluate whether you are creating a culture where people have the resources, time, and space for insight and creative problem-solving.

Did you know that there's a direct connection between your positivity and happiness and how creative you are at any time? In her book, *Positivity*, Dr. Fredrickson explains the "broaden effect": "Positivity broadens our minds and expands our range of vision." Research has shown that positivity expands our minds in various ways. It also has been found to broaden the views we have of ourselves and enables for more connected relationships at work and in our personal lives. Innovation will always be a crucial aspect of leadership, and positivity is proven to support you by enabling you to consistently create new ideas.

Belief in Yourself

My intention is for you to believe in your strengths, your resilience, and your capabilities. Remind yourself of the tremendous value that you bring to your teams, your boss, and your organization. You wouldn't have the position that you have now if people didn't believe in you. Believe in yourself and believe in your intentions, your abilities, and your experience. Never lose sight of your big dreams and know that they will shift and change. When you are working towards purposeful and meaningful goals, the journey becomes the end, and the goal becomes the means. What this means is that you experience contentment, joy, excitement, and many other pleasurable emotions during the process of moving toward your goals. You do not need to wait until you achieve the goal to feel happy and satisfied. Trust yourself and trust the process. Life is an amazing journey when you are connected and accepting of who you are.

When challenges arise, you can become stronger because of them and grow. This has been proven by Achor's concept of "falling up." Every new action and opportunity can enable you to see yourself in a different light. Self-perception theory in psychology has proven that we perceive ourselves based on our actions, just as we perceive others based on theirs. High-performance coach Burchard, who is also a *New York Times* bestselling author, states, "Get more competent by gathering knowledge, skills, and abilities in the areas you are passionate about. More competence equals more confidence." Each time that you overcome an obstacle, you perceive yourself as stronger and more resilient. When you are in a leadership position, you've been given the opportunity to change people's lives! Be the person that your boss, peers, family, and teams need you to be.

Positive psychology demonstrates that our genetic history, life circumstances, and daily choices all contribute to how happy we are. We make roughly 35,000 choices a day! Choosing to master and prioritize a healthy mindset is key to your success! Tony Hsieh chose to walk away from millions of dollars to live with passion and stay true to who he is. This shift enabled him to create the company and culture of his dreams. Prioritize your self-development and never stop growing. Your professional happiness is directly linked to how much you are evolving as a leader and as a person. Keep an open mind to the ideas of others and incorporate the mindset of "how can we make this work?" Creativity breeds happiness, and happiness increases creativity. Having a bias towards innovation will make work more enjoyable and enable you to create a team culture that outshines the competition. Believe in yourself and be the happy leader!

You have now learned my eight steps to being a happy and wildly successful leader. If you understand and implement all of them, you will be unstoppable!

Happy Leader Prompts

1. Choose the daily rituals that you want to commit to in order to support a healthy mindset and schedule them in your calendar.

2. Choose an area of yourself that you want to develop personally or professionally and sign up for a course or class.

3. Starting today, pause before saying no to someone or something at work. Create space to have an open mind and be excited about creativity.

CHAPTER 14:

The Ripple Effect

I t was a warm spring evening in Istanbul, where I was the director of marketing and public relations for the W Istanbul Hotel. The senior vice president of luxury brands for Starwood Hotels, Eva Ziegler, and her director were in the city for a project on which I had worked for 10 months. One of the brand pillars of W Hotels is design, and I had created a design competition for university students across Turkey. All the applicants had designed innovative additions for the guestrooms at the W Istanbul Hotel. It was an online submission and application process, and I had created a partnership with Istanbul Design Week for the competition. The global brand team had selected the winner and runner-up, who would each win cash prizes and accolades. Up until this point, no one around the world had led and executed a university design competition. We had also brought in other W design teams from Asia who were exhibiting at the show. I was filled with excitement and pride on the day when we could announce the winners onstage at Istanbul Design Week.

Eva and her director arrived from Istanbul in the afternoon and came straight to the hotel. They freshened up, and then the three of us hopped in a taxi to go to the show. Istanbul is always full of traffic, and that day was no different. Eva was due to be onstage at 4:30 in the afternoon, and time was running out. We finally arrived at the location across the city and hopped out of the cab. We entered the exhibition gates and looked at the map in my hands. The exhibition hall, where Eva was due to be in minutes, was clear across the grounds. The three of us looked at each other and began to sprint through the crowd and exhibition tents.

We arrived at the tall, white tent and pushed through the jam-packed audience to get to the front. Once we connected Eva with the show director, we made our way partly back to the audience. Eva was due to go onstage in minutes. My heart was pounding from the sprint, and I could hardly catch my breath. Over 600 people were packed in the tent and ready to hear about the brand project that I had created. The humming of the crowd's voices buzzed loudly in my ears. I kept looking around over everyone's heads, thinking, "This place is packed!" They then announced Eva's name, and our brand words and colors flashed onto the enormous screen behind the stage. She walked onstage, still looking a little flush from our mad dash. The crowd roared with applause to welcome her. The brand director and I looked at each other beaming—it was way too cool.

Eva gave a fascinating talk on the history of W Hotels and its commitment to design and creativity. Then it was time to call the contest's winner and runner-up to the stage. The two students walked onstage, and I was filled with pleasure and joy. I will remember the look on their faces for the rest of my life. Eva told the story of the competition and how students from across Turkey had entered. She then showed their design submissions on the huge screen, and the crowd roared with applause. My body was covered in goose bumps—it was one of the best moments of my career. Press snapped pictures as the students accepted their certificates and prizes. The W Hotel hadn't always been welcomed in the 2,500-year-old city. Yet, here we were, deeply connecting the brand to university students and the Turkish design world. It was unbelievable!

That night we had a roaring party at the W Lounge back at the hotel. Turkish celebrities, journalists, and the elite of Istanbul were all there. A famous DJ kept everyone dancing until the early hours of the morning, and the entire hotel was buzzing. I might as well have been wearing a dress with the word "Proud" written across the front. I didn't stop grinning until after I returned home to go to sleep. All the hard work, challenges, and bumps along the way had been well worth it.

The very next day, we set Eva up in our Extreme Wow Suite for a series of interviews with top design, lifestyle, business, and travel publications. It was a fantastic day for press and a strong way to finish her two-day trip to the city. At the end of the second day, I recall standing at the front hotel door with my husband and thanking Eva for coming. She squeezed me tightly and shook our hands. She smiled and exclaimed, "Congratulations, Tia! What a huge success for the W Istanbul and for our brand." Then she turned and got into the little yellow taxi and left. The design competition and Istanbul Design Week partnership began as a pipe dream in my head. Yet it had been executed with astounding results!

The successful W Istanbul Design Week Brand partnership symbolizes to me overcoming challenges and creating professional relationships. While I was out of my comfort and experience zones in many ways, I found success through creativity, optimism, and determination. You might be in a position right now that's presenting you with a long list of obstacles and aren't sure if you have what it takes. Those thoughts and insecurities are normal and are a natural aspect of your professional development. Life would be boring if you were comfortable all the time at work! When you're working towards goals that align with you and that you are passionate about, the journey is incredible. As long as you're leading people with effort, there will always be bumps along the road traveled. Accept that these exist and become wiser because of them.

We are told how to be happy. You and I learn how to live and view the world by our parents, family members and friends, and from how society tells us to view it. We are influenced by our cultures and where we grew up. We are constantly shown messages by the media. Society tells us how to be happy, but the incredible fact is that we now *know* what makes us happier. Positive psychologists from around the world have been studying happy people and both painful and pleasant emotions. Their research and the methodologies are vastly different from those of the self-help movement. While the self-help movement tells people to just believe, to know "the secret," and to think positively, the research by the positive psychologists is about the mind, body, and spirit. What you might have learned about what makes you happy up until now could be wrong, and that's okay. What I want you to know is that there are so many personal happiness resources available to you, and this body of research keeps growing. If you are truly serious about your happiness and well-being, the science of happiness is there waiting for you and is one of life's greatest gifts. You are not stuck! Your choices matter, and the daily choices you make can increase your spiritual, physical, intellectual, relational, and emotional well-being.

My purpose for writing this book is to positively impact as many leaders around the globe as possible. I cannot reach every company and group in person or virtually with my talks, training programs, and executive retreats, but I can reach them with this book. We all spend a significant part of our lives at work and working, and how we feel and lead while we are there is extremely important. Life is short. None of us knows what will happen tomorrow, and I believe that we deserve to be happy. The happiness movement, the science of happiness, and adult neuroscience are changing the way people and organizations view happiness. It's proven that a direct connection exists between your happiness and your professional success. As a leader, you affect the lives of many people in your organization. How you treat them affects not only how they feel, but it affects their family as well. You have the responsibility to show up positively, and I am here as your guide. I don't have all of the answers, but this book has detailed my exact mindset and methodology. You can thrive personally and achieve killer business results if you incorporate them into your life!

What could be more important than knowing how to prioritize and live a happy life? What could be more important than showing you the exact method on how to be successful in your career and authentically happy as a leader? Imagine if all the leaders in all sectors around the globe prioritized their happiness and chose to be a happy leader at work. Just think about how many people would be positively affected!

Work doesn't have to be draining and stressful, nor does leadership have to be overwhelming and extremely challenging. You must really want to lead other people—it's the first step and you cannot move forward successfully without it. If you don't get energy from leading others and teams, I highly suggest changing career paths and finding a track that does give you energy. So many people are promoted into leadership positions because they are amazing at their job, but it doesn't mean that they will be successful leaders. Leadership is about passion and human connection, and about steering your team into a brighter future. You can read research about what does (and doesn't) make people happy at work. Studies have shown that working too much doesn't equal huge productivity gains. When your personal life is suffering, your work life will also. Everything in life is interconnected. When you take care of your mental and physical health, you are stronger at work and leading people. When you foster and grow your personal relationships, your professional ones will blossom alongside. When you take time off regularly and spend time in nature and exploring your home country and the world, your imagination flourishes. Work can be balanced, fun, joyful, exciting, and amusing!

It's vital to act now because, unfortunately, many aspects of our lives make it more difficult to be happy in life and at work. Technology separates us from work, and the addictive nature of social media has us checking our phones over 2,500 times a day, according to *Inc.* magazine. The media continue to take advantage of our brain's negativity bias and bombard us with negative stories 24 hours a day—it's impossible to escape it. The world is competitive, and people want to get ahead for themselves and their families. The majority of the wealthy countries around the world have unbalanced demands for the hours that people work each week. It's up to you to take charge of your own personal happiness—now. Your friends, family, and coworkers all depend on it. What happens if you don't change and continuously grow? It's not an option. You are responsible for creating a massive, positive ripple effect, and I know you can do it.

Purpose truly matters. Don't give up until you find an industry and career that gives you meaning. Spend time understanding what you are getting from your current role. It isn't enough to have a great title, salary, and benefits package. You must feel that you are contributing or gaining some meaning in one or more ways. Do you get meaning from mentoring and coaching? Do you get meaning from promoting people from within? Do you get meaning from providing jobs and a livelihood to others? Do you get meaning from how your organization is helping to make society or the planet a better place to live? I was lucky in that I discovered at the age of 20 an industry that gave me tremendous meaning. Travel and hospitality have given me so many gifts, both personally and professionally. Remember, your work doesn't have to be filled with meaningful and purposeful activities every single day. It is about finding, acknowledging, and being connected to what does.

Be a lifelong learner. Not only will it make you happier, but it will make you more successful. Leadership is a science and an art. Continually experiment to find what works the best for you. Each environment and team will call for you to flex, grow, and adapt. You now have all the strategies and tactics you need. Try them and let me know how you are doing. I truly want you to thrive at work and have your teams reap the benefits. As you are learning and growing along the way, you need support. All great leaders in the world have a tribe that enables them to stand tall and keep growing. You can absolutely be all that you want to be.

The number one takeaway that I want you to remember is this:

HAPPY LEADERS ARE MORE SUCCESSFUL.

Happy leaders are more productive, engaged, and creative! Happy leaders create loyal employees and attract the best talent.

Happy leaders receive more promotions, perks, and bonuses. Happy people live longer! Happy people have stronger relationships and less health challenges and are what the world needs now more than ever! Happy people are more generous. Humanity desperately needs more kindness and generosity.

Thank you for coming along on this journey with me. I value you and your time, and I know that you truly care; otherwise, you would not have chosen to read this book. We are now forever connected, and I am honored to be a part of your life. You have my exact happy living and happy leading methodology. You are going to be amazing!

Become the Happy Leader. The world needs you to help it become a happier and more compassionate place.

ABOUT THE AUTHOR

Tia Graham is A Certified Chief Happiness Officer and the founder of Arrive At Happy. She has worked with dozens of global companies, such as Four Seasons, Hilton Hotels, and The American Heart Association, to elevate engagement and drive bottom-line results. Holding multiple certifications in neuroscience, positive psychology, coaching, and employee morale, she has supported numerous leaders and employees in moving their businesses forward. Prior to running Arrive At Happy, Tia led sales and marketing teams at luxury hotels in the United States and Europe for brands like W Hotels, Westin, and the London.

Tia has a business degree in tourism from the University of Hawaii and is widely regarded by the corporate happiness community. She is a speaker at the annual World Happiness Summit. Her insights have been featured in national publications like *Forbes*, *CNN*, *THRIVE Global*, *The Los Angeles Times*, and *Well + Good*. She partners with business executives to elevate engagement, productivity, revenue, and innovation utilizing her evidence based Business Accelerator Program.

Connect with Tia Graham:
tia@arriveathappy.com
www.arriveathappy.com

ENDNOTES

1   Amit Kumar, Matthew A. Killingsworth, and Thomas Gilovich, "Waiting for Merlot: Anticipatory Consumption of Experiential and Material Purchases," *Journal of Psychological Science* 25, no. 10 (August 21, 2014).

2   Thomas Gilovich, Amit Kumar, and Lily Jampol, "A Wonderful Life: Experiential Consumption and the Pursuit of Happiness," *Journal of Consumer Psychology* 25, no. 1 (September 19, 2014).

3   Elizabeth W. Dunn, Lara B. Aknin, and Michael I. Norton, "Prosocial Spending and Happiness: Using Money to Benefit Others Pays Off," *Current Directions in Psychological Science* 23, no. 41 (February 3, 2014).

4   Angus Deaton and Daniel Kahneman, "High Income Improves Evaluation of Life but Not Emotional Well-being," *Proceedings of the National Academy of Sciences of the United States of America* 107, no. 38 (September 21, 2010).

5   Sonja Lyubomirsky, Laura King, and Ed Diener, "The Benefits of Frequent Positive Affect: Does Happiness Lead to Success?" *The American Psychology Association, Psychological Bulletin* 131, no. 6 (November 2005).

6   A. Keller, K. Litzelman, L. E. Wisk, T. Maddox, E. R. Cheng, P. D. Creswell, and W. P. Witt, "Does the Perception That Stress Affects Health Matter? The Association with Health and

Mortality," *Health Psychology* 31, no. 5 (2012): 677–684

7 Amy Adkins, "Only 35% of U.S. Managers Are Engaged in Their Jobs," *Gallup*, April 2, 2015

8 Clément S. Bellet, Jan-Emmanuel De Neve, and George Ward. "Does Employee Happiness Have an Impact on Productivity?," CEP Discussion Papers dp1655, Centre for Economic Performance, LSE, 2019.

9 Andrew Chamberlain and Daniel Zhao, "Happy Employees, Satisfied Customers: The Link Between Glassdoor Reviews and Customer Satisfaction," *Glassdoor Economic Research Report* (August 7, 2019).

10 Bradley Owens, Wayne E. Baker, and Kim S. Cameron, "Relational Energy at Work: Implications for Job Engagement and Job Performance," *Journal of Applied Psychology* 101, no. 1 (2011): 35–49.

11 Kendall Cotton Bronk, Patrick L. Hill, Daniel K. Lapsley, Tasneem L. Talib, and Holmes Finch, "Purpose, Hope, and Life Satisfaction in Three Age Groups," *The Journal of Positive Psychology* 4, no. 6 (2009): 500–510

12 John Ratey and Eric Hageman, *Spark: The Revolutionary New Science of Exercise and the Brain* (New York: Little, Brown and Company, 2008).

13 H. R. Colten, and B. M. Altevogt, *Sleep Disorders and Sleep Deprivation: An Unmet Public Health Problem*, ed. Institute of Medicine (US) Committee on Sleep Medicine and Research (Washington, DC: National Academies Press, 2006).

14 S. K. Nelson-Coffey, P. M. Ruberton, J. Chancellor, J. E. Cornick, J. Blascovich, S. Lyubomirsky. The Proximal Experience of Awe. *PLoS ONE* 14, no. 5 (2019): e0216780.

15 T. M. Amabile and S. J. Kramer, "Inner Work Life: Understanding the Subtext of Business Performance," *Harvard*

Business Review 85, no.5 (2007):72–144.

16   P. A. Mueller and D. M. Oppenheimer, "The Pen Is Mightier than the Keyboard: Advantages of Longhand over Laptop Note Taking [published correction appears in *Psychological Science* 29, no. 9 (September 2018: 1565–1568]. Psychological Science 25, no. 6 (2014): 1159–1168. doi:10.1177/0956797614524581.

17   M. Mattson, K. Moehl, N. Ghena, et al. "Intermittent Metabolic Switching, Neuroplasticity and Brain Health, *Nature Reviews Neuroscience* 19 (2018): 81–94, https://doi.org/10.1038/nrn.2017.156.

18   Rick Fulwiler, "Using Effective Listening to Improve Leadership in Environmental Health and Safety," *Harvard T.H. Chan School of Public Health* (August 2018).

19   L. C. Hone, A. Jarden, S. Duncan, and G. M. Schofield, "Flourishing in New Zealand Workers: Associations with Lifestyle Behaviors, Physical Health, Psychosocial, and Work-related Indicators, *Journal of Occupational and Environmental Medicine* 57, no. 9 (2015): 973–983.

20   R. A. Gotink, R. Meijboom, M. W. Vernooij, M. Smits, and M. G. Hunink, "Eight-Week Mindfulness Based Stress Reduction Induces Brain Changes Similar to Traditional Long-term Meditation Practice—A Systematic Review," *Brain and Cognition* 108 (2016): 32–41, doi:10.1016/j.bandc.2016.07.001.

21   Charles Duhigg, "What Google Learned from Its Quest to Build the Perfect Team," *The New York Times*, February 25, 2016.

22   Teresa M. Amabile and Steven Kramer. 2011. *The Progress Principle* (Boston, MA: Harvard Business Review Press).

23   Barbara Fredrickson, *Positivity: Discover the Upward Spiral That Will Change Your Life* (New York: Harmony, 2009).

24   Kim Cameron, *Positive Leadership: Strategies for Extraordinary Performance* (San Francisco: Berrett-Koehler Publishers, 2012).

25   Herminia Ibarra, "The Most Productive Way to Develop as a Leader," *Harvard Business Review*, March 27, 2015.

26   Shawn Achor, *The Happiness Advantage: The Seven Principles of Positive Psychology That Fuel Success and Performance at Work* (Red Fern, New South Wales, Australia: Currency 2010).

A free ebook edition is available with the purchase of this book.

To claim your free ebook edition:

1. Visit MorganJamesBOGO.com
2. Sign your name CLEARLY in the space
3. Complete the form and submit a photo of the entire copyright page
4. You or your friend can download the ebook to your preferred device

Print & Digital Together Forever.

| Snap a photo | Free ebook | Read anywhere |

CPSIA information can be obtained
at www.ICGtesting.com
Printed in the USA
JSHW021450221022
32010JS00001B/4